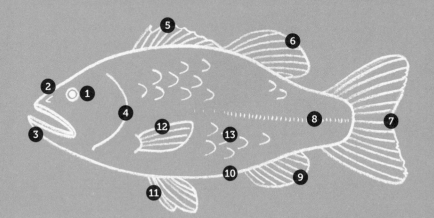

1. EYE
2. NOSTRILS
3. MOUTH
4. GILL COVER
5. SPINY DORSAL FIN
6. SOFT DORSAL FIN
7. CAUDAL (TAIL) FIN
8. LATERAL LINE
9. ANAL FIN
10. VENT
11. PELVIC FINS
12. PECTORAL FINS
13. SCALES

A Visual Guide to
Sushi-Making at Home

A Visual Guide to

Sushi-Making at Home

Hiro Sone and Lissa Doumani

Photographs by Antonis Achilleos

CHRONICLE BOOKS

SAN FRANCISCO

Library of Congress Cataloging-in-Publication Data available.

ISBN 978-1-4521-0710-3

Manufactured in China

MIX
Paper from
responsible sources
FSC® C008047

Designed by **Vanessa Dina**
Prop styling by **Christine Wolheim**
Food styling by **Hiro Sone and Lissa Doumani**
Typesetting by **DC Type**

The authors wish to thank Susan Naderi Johnston for her help with the What to Drink with Sushi text.

10 9 8 7 6 5 4 3 2 1

Chronicle Books LLC
680 Second Street
San Francisco, California 94107
www.chroniclebooks.com

Acknowledgments

Having grown up on a small rice farm, I appreciate the hard work that goes into growing rice. Long and backbreaking hours are spent planting the rice, harvesting it, and hoping the weather does not destroy the crop. Without rice farmers we would not have this critical ingredient in sushi-making.
—Hiro

We would like to first thank the fishermen who go out each and every day—tirelessly—to bring back the bounty of the sea that allows us to make such beautiful sushi. Theirs is a hard life with limited rewards for them but boundless rewards for all of us who consume their fish. We hope that by working together we can keep their profession viable for them and for the oceans they draw from.

A big thank you to Tom Worthington of Monterey Fish, who kept us on track with information and tirelessly answered all of our questions—and there are so many factors to consider when writing about fish, from availability to nomenclature! He has been providing us with the highest quality fish since we opened our first restaurant, Terra.

Thank you to Lorena Jones, who had the crazy notion to ask a couple of non–sushi chefs to create a book that could be understood by cooks of all levels, and for the patience she showed when we went so deeply into understanding the anatomy of fish and how to break them down.

Thanks also to Sarah Billingsley, who edited a book that was so very technical on a subject that was not familiar to her. She showed angelic patience when we came back time and time again to correct the small details that mean so much to us. Many times we all ended up laughing at where things got crossed up.

Vanessa Dina was able to interpret our vision so beautifully; her patience and gentle guidance has brought together a stunning book. Thank you also to the rest of the team at Chronicle Books.

To the sushi lovers: Yes, you. We are one with you and love the passion and exuberance you have for sushi. You have helped sushi become one of the most important cuisines in the world. To feed our passion, let's think about sustainability and respect the land and the oceans we are a part of.
—Lissa and Hiro

Sushi Rolls (Maki-zushi)

Sushi Bowls (Sushi Don)
and Other Types of Sushi

Introduction

Sushi. When you hear that word, be honest; don't you immediately ask yourself, Where can I go to eat sushi right now? Fortunately, sushi is widely available these days, especially in larger cities. But even in smaller towns, you are likely to find at least a few Japanese restaurants, and most of them will have a couple of sushi items on the menu.

This is a dramatic change from just thirty years ago when sushi was popular only among travelers and cooks and diners interested in ethnic cuisines. Now, you can find sushi in your local grocery store, something that you don't even see in small markets in Japan. In bigger U.S. cities, you can usually find a Japanese restaurant within a square block or two of any commercial district. Upscale Western-style eateries have started to put sashimi on their menus, though most of them are not yet ready to add

rice to the mix by trying to serve sushi. At Ame, we fall into this category. One section of our menu is devoted to sashimi, though it is not at all traditionally prepared but instead influenced by the world's cuisines.

We go out for sushi and sashimi at least once a week but usually twice. It is what we crave and what leaves us feeling well afterward. We are traditionalists, preferring pristine fish and a small accompaniment when appropriate, though we do enjoy watching the twists that sushi chefs have been putting on traditional sushi varieties. These culinary masters have a natural curiosity that makes them want to grow and create. Some new ideas work; other times, too many ingredients are used and the fish gets lost. Not surprisingly, this happens most frequently with sushi rolls.

Although, nowadays, diners in the United States can choose from

many Japanese restaurants, big and small, plain and fancy, such abundance is relatively recent. In the years preceding World War II, Japanese eating establishments were primarily simple spots located in Japanese American neighborhoods in towns in Hawaii and on the West Coast. In the 1930s, New York boasted a handful of restaurants that catered to cosmopolitan diners who enjoyed tempura, teriyaki, and other unchallenging fare, but not sushi or sashimi. It was only after the war that Japanese restaurants began appearing in greater numbers, and it was not until the late 1950s that sushi was on the menu.

Originally, only a handful of rolls (*maki-zushi*) were served: tuna, cucumber, marinated *kampyō* (dried gourd strips), and *futomaki* (a thicker roll usually without raw fish). Back then (and still at some places today), sushi was served on a large wooden boat. It is not clear why a boat was used, unless it was to telegraph subconsciously that the fish was fresh from the sea. The now-famous California roll was invented in the 1960s at Tokyo Kaikan, a Japanese restaurant in downtown Los Angeles. The chef was trying to create sushi like he had made in Japan but using ingredients available in his new home. Crab was plentiful but it needed something rich to complement it, so he tried avocado. The California roll was not an instant success, but it eventually developed a following, and it illustrates how sushi chefs worked with what was available.

California rolls did not make it to Japan until the 1980s, and even then they appeared at only a few restaurants. Sushi chefs at some establishments in the United States are purists and still refuse to make them. But most people in America enjoy a balance between traditional and contemporary sushi, and even the rolls that we consider over the top with ingredients have their own following.

Almost all cultures include raw fish at their table. For example, the Italians have *pesce crudo*, the French *poisson cru*, and the Peruvians ceviche. During our travels outside of the United States, we have seen many versions of sushi. At a popular sushi bar in Cabo San Lucas, Mexico, the offerings maintain a strong Japanese tradition but include traditional Mexican flavors such as chiles and occasionally an accompanying salsa.

In San Sebastián, Spain, a chef served us Spanish molecular cuisine–influenced sushi, marking the first time we experienced soy sauce foam.

Peru already had a long history of eating raw fish when Japanese immigrants began arriving at the beginning of the twentieth century, so today Peruvian cuisine carries a prominent Japanese culinary mark, and local menus often describe dishes as being *Nikkei*, or in the Japanese style. This is especially evident in Peruvian ceviches and *tiraditos* (raw fish with a spicy sauce). In a sushi bar in the Marche region of Italy, we have eaten fish marinated in extra-virgin olive oil.

The biggest difference we have seen between Japanese raw fish cuisine in the United States and elsewhere in the world is that people in other countries seem to prefer sashimi over sushi. Both sashimi and sushi are prepared, but the variety and interest on the plate are focused on a passion for the fish alone, whereas Americans tend to favor the combination of fish and rice.

We enjoy observing and sampling the creativity of sushi chefs and how they adapt their local fish and products to their sushi-making. As noted earlier, sometimes these innovations work, and sometimes it is hard for us to say, "That's sushi." But even if we question whether a particular dish can accurately be called sushi, we are always interested in expanding our concept of what sushi can be and where sushi may go.

· · ·

This book is your introduction to making sushi at home, a prospect that may at first seem daunting but is actually easily achieved with a little practice. We have included tips on selecting the highest-quality fish and shellfish—the only type that should be used for sushi—and explicit instructions on how to break down a wide variety of seafood, information that will prove useful for other applications as well, such as yielding fillets from a whole fish to grill or fry. Of course, sometimes you may want to make sushi without all the work of breaking down each fish, or you may not want such a large amount of fish, so we

have provided separate instructions on how to properly cut for sushi a portion of fish that you have purchased at the market. This gives you the freedom to buy smaller pieces and enjoy a much larger selection for one night of sushi-making.

Some types of sushi that we have included will be familiar to you. Others you will have never tried or even considered. For example, we have put our own style on some of the more unusual offerings, like Nigiri with Olive Oil–marinated Sardines (page 142); included some of the funkier sushi we like, like those made with *natto* (fermented soybeans) or with cod milt; and have highlighted a style we particularly enjoy, vegetarian sushi. Rolls are a challenge to novice sushi makers, but our step-by-step photos should help simplify the task for you. Finally, we have a good assortment of sushi bowls, the easiest sushi of all to master: scoop sushi rice

into a bowl, lay sliced fish and/or vegetables on top, and sit down and eat.

We have strong opinions about what to drink with sushi and have included our observations on how to choose the correct beer, sake, shōchū, and wine. Although we do not recommend specific brands because availability varies from region to region, we do provide the information you will need to have an intelligent conversation with a store clerk when you shop. Our sections on ingredients, condiments and garnishes, and tools and equipment will help you outfit your pantry and *batterie de cuisine* for all the techniques and recipes that follow.

What we hope that you get from this book is the determination to make sushi—that the fear of breaking down a fish or making the perfect pot of sushi rice does not defeat you. Your first attempt will be difficult, but we can promise you that every experience after that will be much easier.

A Short History of Sushi

The story of sushi is very different from what most people think. Around 400 B.C. in Southeast Asia, people started to preserve fish by encasing salted cleaned fish in cooked rice and leaving it to ferment for several months. This technique, which prevented the fish from spoiling, traveled from Southeast Asia through China and then to Japan in the Heian period (794–1185). This was not yet sushi; instead it was simply a way to preserve fish. When it was time to eat the fish, it was removed from the rice and the rice was thrown away.

In the Muromachi period (1336–1573), a change occurred in the processing of fish. Instead of fully "cooking" the fish during the fermentation process, the fish was eaten when it was only partially cured, before it had changed flavor and texture completely. People also started eating the slightly cured rice, which was a bit sour, though the rice and fish were eaten separately.

Sushi as we know it today began in the Edo period (1603–1868; Edo is the old name for Tokyo). By now, the Japanese had developed a taste for slightly soured fish and rice, and vinegar was introduced to the preparation. Fish was quickly cured with vinegar and salt, to maintain its freshness and texture, and a little vinegar was mixed into the cooked rice to give it the pleasant taste that people had grown to like. Edo-style sushi was always made with lightly vinegared and cured fish, though the amount of time a particular type of fish was cured varied, with some cured for as briefly as an hour and others for as long as several days. The vinegar acted as a natural preservative, killing any unwanted bacteria and allowing the fish to be kept longer. The Edo period was also when sushi first took the form of a piece of fish laid over an oblong mound of rice, a style known as *nigiri-zushi* that debuted in the early nineteenth century and was sold by street vendors.

Today, high-quality fish for sushi is available on a daily basis, so preserving fish is no longer necessary. If vinegared fish is used for sushi nowadays, it is because its taste is desired—a taste that harks back to the Edo period.

Sushi Styles and a Word on Sashimi

There are five basic styles of sushi: *nigiri-zushi*, *maki-zushi*, *inari-zushi*, *chirashi-zushi*, and *oshi-zushi*. Most sushi falls into one of these styles.

Nigiri-zushi (hand-formed sushi) is an individual piece of fish on an oblong pad of rice.

Gunkan-maki (warship roll) is a nigiri-size pad of rice with nori wrapped around the exterior to hold a topping, such as *ikura* (salmon roe) or *uni* (sea urchin), in place.

Temari-zushi (ball sushi), yet another type of nigiri, is made by pairing a small scoop of rice and a slice of fish or vegetable (either must be pliable) and tightening them together in a piece of cloth or plastic wrap to form a ball. When the sushi is unwrapped and served, it resembles a flower.

Maki-zushi is a long roll of rice with one or more fillings, wrapped with nori. This rolled sushi, which is highly popular in Japan and the United States, includes *hosomaki* (skinny roll), *futomaki* (large roll), *temaki* (hand roll), and *uramaki* (inside-out roll; that is, rice on the outside), among other bowls.

Inari-zushi is almost always just sushi rice in a pouch made of fried tofu (*aburagé*), but for festive occasions, some cooked vegetables or a few small shrimp may also be included. We have slipped a recipe for this homey favorite into the chapter on sushi rolls.

Chirashi-zushi refers to a composed sushi in a vessel. It is usually a combination of assorted raw fish and other items artistically placed on sushi rice in a *donburi* (bowl) or lacquer box. *Gomoku-zushi*, which is similar, includes cooked or raw fish and vegetables (usually these pieces are smaller than those in the *chirashi-zushi*) mixed into sushi rice. *Gomoku* refers to the use of five ingredients (*go* means "five"), though the number of ingredients is not strictly adhered to.

Oshi-zushi (pressed sushi) originates in the Osaka area and is made with a special rectangular mold widely available at Japanese shops. The fish is put into the mold, topped with sushi rice, and firmly pressed. The block is released from the mold and cut into bite-size pieces for serving. This sushi style typically uses vinegared or cooked fish.

Sashimi

Although the making and serving of sashimi does not appear in these pages, it is so closely linked with sushi that we feel a brief discussion is appropriate here. Technically, all fish that can be served as sushi can be served as sashimi. Many chefs believe that not all fish are equally suited to both presentations, however. For example, some chefs feel that the fattiest slices of fish need to be served with rice to balance their rich flavor and texture.

It is also surprisingly difficult to describe how to prepare sashimi, even though it is nothing more than unadorned, unseasoned sliced raw fish. That's because its success depends on the ability of the chef to cut it properly, which comes only with knowledge. The chef must *know* the fish—the direction of the muscles, the texture of the flesh—in order to slice it in a manner that complements the fish and heightens the experience of the eater.

One of the most beautiful sashimi presentations is when a firm white fish fillet is used for making *usuzukuri*, or paper-thin fish slices. In Japan, the most famous version of this dish is made from fugu (also known as puffer fish), some organs of which are highly poisonous. Halibut is another popular choice. The translucent fish slices are arranged in a flower or fan pattern over an ornate plate. When done properly, the design of the plate shows through the translucent fish slices. Garnished with short lengths of fresh chive and *momiji oroshi* (spicy grated daikon) and served with *ponzu* (soy-citrus sauce) for dipping, this is a very special dish.

Sashimi is a tricky word, as it does not refer only to fish. Sliced raw horse meat is a popular sashimi in Japan (and in Italy). In Japan, chicken tenders are also used for sashimi, usually dipped quickly in hot water just to blanch the exterior. For most Americans, this is a scary thought, but having eaten chicken sashimi many times, we can attest to the fact that it is very good. That said, don't worry, we have not included a recipe for chicken sashimi in this book.

If you have a piece of fish that you can put on rice, you can make sashimi from it. It will not be the absolutely perfect sashimi that you get at a good Japanese restaurant, but it will still be great. Both sushi and sashimi use the same high-quality fish, but as already noted, the fish is cut differently for sashimi for ease of eating and proper texture.

If you want to serve sashimi, you will need a large platter and the beautiful strings of daikon that are traditionally used to support the sashimi. The cutting of daikon takes years to learn and yields many cut fingers in the process. To simplify the task, look for user-friendly tools for cutting the strings at Japanese grocery stores and hardware stores. Or, cut the daikon into very fine julienne and then fluff it a bit to make a small haystack on the plate. Then all you need to do is put a piece of *shiso* (a relative of mint) on the daikon and lay the fish slices against the shiso. If the fish is paired with ponzu, serve the sauce in small bowls on the side. Other garnishes, such as momiji oroshi (see page 121), can be put directly next to the fish they are to accompany. The idea is to present the fish selection beautifully and with the proper condiments. A good place to start is the recipe for chirashi-zushi on page 212; imagine those ingredients arranged on a platter instead of on a bowl of rice. Always accompany sashimi with soy sauce and wasabi.

Choosing Fish and Shellfish

The most important thing to remember when making or ordering sushi is that the best-quality fish and shellfish must be used. To help you make your selections, talk to your fishmonger, talk to a sushi chef, and think about what is in season. In this book, we explain how to pick a fresh fish and other creatures of the sea. If what you buy is good, what you make will be good regardless of the presentation. We may eat with our eyes, but we enjoy with our taste buds.

One of the key aspects of selection is sustainability. We all must be aware of what is happening to the waters, both near and far, that provide us with the means to make sushi. Poor fisheries management has taken a toll on what Mother Nature has supplied. We need to educate ourselves on what impact current fishing practices are having on our environment. Engaging your fishmonger in conversation to discover what is in season, what is wild, and what is sustainably farmed is critical to making sound choices. Over-fishing, unregulated fishing, habitat destruction, poor fishing gear selection, and improper aquaculture methods all threaten sustainability, and becoming a knowledgeable shopper can reduce the impact of these damaging practices.

Many online sources exist to help you stay informed on these issues. But what is available where you live and your personal taste cannot be accommodated on any single website. Each person and each business needs to make individual decisions on what to buy. Following are a few of the many agencies that post important information on fish and shellfish sustainability on their websites. Refer to them and work with your fishmonger to acquire the best that is offered in your area. If your fishmonger does not carry a fish that you want, he or she may be able to order it for you, so always take the time to ask.

National Oceanic and Atmospheric Administration (NOAA) FishWatch
www.fishwatch.gov

Food and Agriculture Organization (FAO) of the United Nations Fisheries and Aquaculture Department
www.fao.org/fishery

Blue Ocean Institute
www.blueocean.org/programs/sustainable-seafood-program

Marine Stewardship Council (MSC)
www.msc.org

Monterey Bay Aquarium Seafood Watch
www.montereybayaquarium.org/cr/seafoodwatch.aspx

University of Rhode Island (URI) Sustainable Seafood Initiative
www.seagrant.gso.uri.edu/sustainable_seafood

Sushi Etiquette

Although this book is about sushi, we have included a bit of sashimi etiquette here, as well, since both are served at sushi bars. The accompaniments for sushi and sashimi are fairly standard, but they can be elevated by the talent or curiosity of the sushi chef. In general, the fish will be smeared on the underside with wasabi by the chef before it is placed on the rice, and the sushi will be accompanied by soy sauce. Many sushi chefs make their own seasoned soy sauce called *sushijouyu* or *murasaki*. The use of the latter term, which means "purple," dates from the Meiji period (1868–1912), when it was coined in reference to the deep color of the sauce. If a piece of sushi should have an additional seasoning, the chef will add it to the top. You should add nothing more.

Always listen to the chef. For example, he may tell you not to dip the sushi into soy sauce because he has seasoned the fish. On the *geta* (named after a Japanese shoe that it resembles), the bamboo or wooden board on which the sushi is served, there will be *gari* (pickled ginger). This is not a salad but a palate cleanser. Also, it should not be dipped into soy sauce for eating, though there is an acceptable technique that calls for using gari to brush soy sauce on the fish, rather than turn the sushi upside down to dunk the fish. For sashimi, the chef covers a plate with fine strands of daikon, props a shiso leaf against the mound of daikon, arranges the fish on the leaf, and puts a small bit of wasabi on the plate.

Since everyone has his or her own way of eating sushi, we will go over the basic etiquette. It is always best to understand the proper way of doing something before you find your own way.

When you first sit down, a server will bring you a towel, traditionally a hot towel on cold days and a cold towel on hot days. Use the towel to wipe your hands lightly and then fold it and leave it on the counter away from you and to the side of the hand that you use to eat. After eating a piece of sushi, clean your fingers that held the sushi by simply brushing them against the towel, without picking the towel up. Some good sushi restaurants prepare special dampened cloths that are folded and placed near you solely for this use.

It is fine to eat sushi with your fingers, though sashimi must be eaten with chopsticks. Do not add wasabi to your soy sauce. If you want a little more wasabi on your sushi, use your finger or chopsticks to wipe a bit on your fish. For sashimi, pick up a small bit of wasabi, dab it on the fish, and then dip the fish in the soy sauce.

When dipping the sushi in soy sauce, dip the fish side, not the rice side. This is done for two reasons. One, you want to season the fish but not overseason it, and this technique will accomplish that. Two, if you dip the rice into the soy, the rice will fall apart all over you and into your soy sauce container.

Ideally, you should eat the piece of sushi in one bite. The portion has been created so its complete flavor is realized only if it is consumed in a single mouthful. Personal experience has taught us that this is not always true or possible, however, so don't worry if you have to take two bites. Before you move on, eat a piece of gari to rinse—or "reset"—your palate.

To enjoy sushi to its fullest, always consider the order in which you eat the fish. Start with the mildest fish, such as halibut, snapper, sea bass, and shrimp. Then move on to fish that is a little richer, including tuna, yellowtail, trout, shellfish, scallop, oyster, clam, or giant clam. Richer still are sardine, mackerel, salmon, and eel, the latter both freshwater and saltwater. Finally, eat the richest fish last: tuna belly, yellowtail belly, sea urchin, and salmon eggs.

The same attention to order is true of rolls. Start with the lighter and move to the richer, saving the most complicated roll for last. We think the best roll to end a meal is *uméboshi* (pickled plum) with shiso, as it is slightly tart and fragrant and acts as a palate cleanser.

These traditional guidelines are a good way for beginners to approach eating sushi. But as with most foods that you encounter and come to enjoy, you will soon find your own way and establish your own order.

What to Drink with Sushi

What you choose to drink with your sushi depends largely on personal taste, of course. Here are the most common beverages offered at sushi bars and how we believe they complement sushi.

Sake

Sake is a fermented alcoholic beverage made from steamed rice, *koji* (steamed rice treated with the special yellow mold *koji-kin*), yeast, and water. People often refer to sake as rice wine, but the process more closely resembles brewing beer. First, the rice is cooked; then it is mixed with the yeast, koji, and water (in three stages); and left to ferment over four days, in the course of which the koji converts the starch molecules of the rice into sugar. Next, the resulting mash is left to sit for three to five weeks, during which time the yeast converts the sugar to alcohol. Sake is the only beverage in which dual fermentation is used in the production. That means that the rice starch is converted to sugar and the sugar is converted to alcohol all in the same brewing tank. It is a wonder that this process was created seventeen hundred years ago.

Most sake has low acidity compared with wine and is low in tannins, too. That's one reason why it is so easy to pair sake with sushi. Plus, eating rice seasoned with rice vinegar while drinking a rice-based beverage strikes us as a natural combination, a way of practicing the often-repeated saying "what grows together goes together."

Four grades of premium sake are excellent for drinking with sushi. They fall under the *ginjo-shu* (*ginjo* sake) umbrella, which refers to sakes brewed with rice, water, the koji mold, yeast, and in some cases a small amount of alcohol. The four grades are *junmai daiginjo-shu*, *junmai ginjo-shu*, *daiginjo-shu*, and *ginjo-shu*. They differ from the less expensive *futsuu-shu* style, which adds alcohol for volume.

In sake-making, the rice primarily impacts the flavor of the sake, and the yeast influences the aroma.

Sake rice, of which there are scores of varieties, has more starch than typical table rice. The emperor of all sake rice varieties is Yamada Nishiki, which is appreciated for its ability to soak up liquid and break down quickly. The flavor of the rice carries through the process into the finished sake, and this flavor works beautifully with the yeast to produce a gorgeous fragrance. Before the rice is used, the outer husk of each kernel is removed, leaving only the inner starch. In general, the more the rice is milled (the milling process is known as *seimaibuai*), or polished, the better the quality of the sake.

For example, junmai daiginjo is made from rice milled to less than 50 percent of its original weight, and junmai ginjo uses rice milled to less than 60 percent. Neither type of sake is manufactured with added distilled alcohol, and both are light and fragrant, with the junmai daiginjo sake more complex and the junmai ginjo sake more refined. If the sake is labeled only *ginjo*, it is made with rice polished to less than 60 percent of its original weight and a small amount of distilled alcohol has been added to heighten the aroma, though not to increase the volume. This typically results in a beverage with a distinguished bouquet and a light touch on the palate. Delicate fish, such as snapper, lightly smoked salmon, ocean trout, and amberjack, pair well with a ginjo sake. Daiginjo sakes, which, like ginjo sakes, include a small amount of distilled alcohol to heighten the aroma, use rice milled to less than 50 percent of its original weight. These sakes have bright aromas, great complexity, and an appreciable elegance. Subtle-flavored fish and shellfish, such as fluke, flounder, halibut, and bay scallops, combine well with these refined sakes.

Junmai-shu, a premium sake outside the ginjo group that contains no added alcohol, uses rice that is milled to less than 70 percent of its original weight. Junmai sakes typically have a full flavor and good acidity and partner well with oily fish like sardines and anchovies and with tempura. They are rich enough to stand up to these flavors, plus the acidity washes away the oiliness of the foods, leaving your mouth ready for the next bite.

Honjozu-shu is a premium sake that uses rice that has been polished to less than 70 percent of its original size, but it contains a very small amount of alcohol to elevate the aroma and flavor. Honjozu sakes can be enjoyed warm or cold and are great with vinegar-marinated fish such as mackerel. A seafood salad dressed with a soy sauce–vinegar base works well with this sake, too.

Several types of sake fall outside the standard sake categories. *Nigori* sake is unfiltered, which means it goes through a very coarse filtration, leaving behind some of the rice lees (fine sediment). It is cloudy white and can range from sweet to dry and from light to creamy to very viscous. Spicy dishes are a nice contrast with nigori sakes, which are often slightly sweet.

Nama sakes, which are produced seasonally, are unpasteurized. Sake is traditionally pasteurized twice, once before bottling and once before storing or shipping. Because nama sakes are sold unpasteurized, they are highly perishable and require refrigeration at all times. These fresh sakes contain wild aromas and are bursting with flavors of fruit and spice. They go well with lighter-flavored fish and sweet shellfish, such as halibut, sea scallops, and shrimp. They also complement various types of Japanese herbs, fruits, and vegetables, such as shiso, yuzu, and daikon.

Yamahai and *kimoto* are sakes made with older hand-production techniques that capture more intense levels of yeast and thus have a particularly gamy, rich flavor and aroma. Foods high in umami, or savory meatiness, complement the natural umami flavors in these two sakes. Although they are not well suited to accompanying sushi, they are good with grilled, stewed, and roasted meats; grilled salmon and richer fish; *natto* (fermented soybeans); and any cut of pork.

Gen-shu is undiluted sake, which just means that no secondary water has been added to dilute the alcohol content. Any grade sake, from *daiginjo* to *honjozu*, can be an undiluted sake, with the difference being that the alcohol content will be between 16 and 20 percent. Gen-shu needs to accompany big flavors that will stand up to the alcohol. Its flavor is not necessarily richer or heavier, however, so it will still go well with sushi. Fatty tuna, monkfish liver, and yellowtail are good matches for the high alcohol content.

Finally, *ko-shu* is aged sake. These sakes are aged by the brewer longer than the typical six to eighteen months of other sakes. This yields a beverage that is richer and darker than younger sakes and has a nutty flavor and a sherrylike quality. These sakes are not meant to go with food. Think of them in the same way you think of sherry or Madeira, and serve them at the end of a meal with cheese or a chocolate dessert.

Unfortunately, despite being armed with information on the different types of sakes, it's often hard to choose sake knowledgeably if you don't read Japanese. Some exporters have added English labels that translate names, identify the importer, and display the federal government alcohol warning disclaimer. These new labels are making discerning different styles easier for shoppers in the Western market.

Ideal temperature

Sake can be consumed at a range of temperatures. The custom of hot sake started in China, where it is believed that warm beverages are healthier for the body than cold. Heat also helped to cover up unpleasant qualities and bitterness in some low-quality sakes. Although some sakes are good consumed warm, especially on a cold winter day, we prefer to drink sake slightly chilled. (The flavors of a premium sake are delicate and heating it will mask them and will release its aromas prematurely.) In general, most premium junmai, ginjo, and daiginjo sakes should be served slightly chilled. Once you have begun drinking sake regularly and exploring the various styles, you will know the best temperature to serve it, according to your own taste.

For chilled sake, you can put the bottle in an ice bucket. For warm sake, you can submerge it in a small vessel in a hot-water bath for five minutes. Be careful the water is not boiling, or it will cause evaporation. Or, you can heat the sake in a microwave. Just make sure that you are fully familiar with your microwave's heating level so the sake does not reach a boil. (If you overheat premium sakes, you risk masking their delicate flavors, or if heated too hot, they will release the aroma that you want to pair with sushi.) Body temperature, known in Japan as *hitohada* (a person's skin temperature, 98.6°F/37°C), is an ideal temperature for warm sake.

How to store and serve sake

How long does sake keep once you have opened the bottle? It starts to oxidize immediately on uncapping, but it generally keeps longer than an uncorked bottle of wine. To increase the shelf life, always refrigerate sake after opening if you don't plan to consume it the same day. An opened bottle can generally be kept from seven days to several weeks. The more delicate sakes will start to lose flavor after about one week, and the fortified sakes, like honjozu, will last a month or more because of their higher alcohol content and because they start with a bigger taste. Beyond that, the sake will begin to go stale and the flavors will soften considerably.

Picking the right drinking vessel for sake is easy. We tell our guests that drinking sake like a fine wine is perfectly acceptable. Wineglasses accentuate aromatics and fit in well with table settings. In Japan and at many American sushi restaurants, *ochoko*, tiny, cylindrical cups, often ceramic, are commonly used. The sake is poured into the cups from a little flask, and because the cups are small, they must be refilled often. Some places use larger tumbler-size cups to cut down on the repeated pourings. The classic porcelain sake cups known as *kiki-choko* are white with two concentric blue circles in the bottom; they come in both the tiny and the tumbler size.

There is no absolute rule for sake serving except the golden rule of enjoying it with others as you pour for others and others pour for you. Never fill your own cup! Pouring for others conveys respect and a show of friendship.

Shōchū

A distilled beverage that can be made from various ingredients, shōchū is most commonly made from barley, buckwheat, rice, or sweet potatoes. In Okinawa, a sugarcane-based shōchū is made, but it is not widely available beyond the island. In the United States, shōchū is most familiar as a substitute for vodka. It is used in cocktails in establishments that lack a liquor license for high-alcohol spirits, though its alcohol level can range anywhere from 25 to 40 percent.

The flavor of shōchū ranges from a light vodka to a midrange whiskey, depending on the producer, the aging process, and the ingredients. In the past, shōchū was consumed by an older population for its health benefits, but it has now been embraced by the younger generation in Japan. An abundance of shōchū bars and brands has appeared, with many of them catering especially to women.

Although shōchū can be imbibed at any temperature, the best way to drink it is straight up or on the rocks, much like you would Scotch or bourbon. That said, it is also consumed a number of other ways, including mixed with

hot or cold oolong tea, mixed with hot water (a drink known as *oyuwari*, a favorite choice in winter months that has a quick impact, much like warm sake), or mixed with soda water and lemon juice, grapefruit juice, or other fruit flavor to make a *chuhai* cocktail. A second cocktail, *umé-chuhai*, which mixes shōchū, soda water, and a few muddled *uméboshi* (pickled plums) and is served on the rocks, is a refreshing, briny accompaniment to tempura sushi rolls. (If you order an umé-chuhai, make sure that it is made with these three ingredients and not with *uméshu*, a popular sweet Japanese liqueur.)

Although people drink what they want when eating sushi, we feel that shōchū straight up and the simpler flavor combinations, with tea, with hot water, or with *umé-chuhai*, are the best choices.

Wine

Matching wine and sushi can be challenging yet fun. You can play off the acids of the sauces and the wine or seek contrasting flavors. Less yeasty styles of sparkling wine work well, as do crisp whites. Austrian Grüner Veltliner is an interesting and refreshing pairing with sushi that contains vegetables, plus it complements wasabi. Delicate white-fleshed fish like fluke, flounder, halibut, and snapper are excellent with fresh, crisp white wines. Two great Italian whites to seek out are Verdicchio and a light Vermentino. The brininess in Vermentino naturally harmonizes with oysters and other saltier preparations. A lighter unoaked Chardonnay also marries well with fish and shellfish

like halibut, albacore, and crab. With spicier dishes, a little residual sugar is good, which means uncorking an off-dry Riesling or Sekt or even a sparkling Chenin Blanc like Vouvray. Bubbles are not just for special occasions.

Pinot Blanc is outstanding with richer seafood such as salmon or squid, as the body holds up to the seafood while the acid cuts through the fat and oiliness. Stewed eel and fattier fish like mackerel or tuna belly work well with light-bodied red wines, such as Pinot Noir, Gamay, and Dolcetto. Avoiding tannins and oaked wine is a must when choosing reds to accompany sushi.

There is no way to find one perfect bottle of wine to match all sushi. It might be fun to try a few different choices by the glass and see what you like. Try every combination possible and have fun!

Beer

Many people like to drink beer with their sushi (it is Hiro's favorite accompaniment), and we have found that a high-quality lager with a great balance of hops, bitterness, and bubbles and an absence of sourness is the ideal choice. Such lagers do not interfere with the delicate taste of the sushi, plus they cleanse and refresh the palate in the same way that green tea does. Ales and dark beers, in contrast, are invariably difficult partners for sushi. They typically contain too many complex flavor characteristics that end up competing with the sushi, and are usually too sweet, too sour, and/or too malty.

Green Tea

In Japan, at the sushi counter, though not at the tables, green tea is usually served in large, thick teacups. This ensures that your meal will not have to be interrupted as often to refill your cup. The tea is also served at a higher temperature than the tea poured at regular Japanese meals, so that it more efficiently rinses the natural fattiness of the fish from your palate. Plus, the tannins in green tea cleanse the palate of strong seafood flavors, preparing it for the next bite of fish.

Outside of sushi bars, green tea is known as *ocha* or *ryokucha*, both traditional Japanese words. But in sushi bars, green tea is called *agari*. Many theories exist as to how this term came about, though we find the following legend the most interesting: During the Edo period, in Japan's red-light districts, tea was served at the beginning of the "service" and again at the end. The first tea was called *ode-bana* (coming flower) and the second tea was *agari-bana* (come-to-the-end flower). This custom moved to sushi bars, where people began to refer to tea served at the end of their meal as *agari*. Over time, the tradition changed yet again, and the tea served at both the beginning and the end of the meal is now called *agari*.

The Sushi Pantry and Tool Kit

Here you will find information on the basic ingredients, condiments and garnishes, and tools and equipment you will need for making and serving the sushi recipes in this book. Many of the items can be found in well-stocked supermarkets or cookware stores. Failing that, seek out hard-to-find ingredients and equipment at a Japanese or Asian shop or online.

Ingredients

Dried bonito shavings, kezuri-bushi

Fillets of bonito, a tunalike member of the mackerel family, are used to make *kezuri-bushi*. The fillets are steamed, smoked, dried to woodlike hardness, and then shaved into flakes. Dried bonito flakes look like pale rose wood shavings and are sold in cellophane packages of different sizes. The shavings come in different sizes, as well: the larger ones (*kezuri-bushi* ⑭) are a basic ingredient of *dashi* (stock), and the smaller ones, *ito-kezuri-bushi* ⑮, finely shredded shavings sometimes known as thread shavings, are used as a garnish. Humidity will ruin kezuri-bushi, so keep in an airtight container.

Kelp for dashi, dashi kombu ⑨

All Japanese kelp belongs to the genus *Laminaria*, and most varieties are harvested off of Japan's large, northern island of Hokkaido. The leaves can be 2 to 12 in/5 to 30.5 cm wide and very long. The harvested kelp is sun-dried and then cut and packaged. Look for cellophane packets labeled *dashi kombu* (kelp for dashi), which typically contain pieces about 4 in/10 cm long. Cost counts when purchasing kombu, and the more expensive the package, the better quality the contents will be. Simply put, this is a good time to spend a little extra money. Once a package is opened, store kombu in a resealable plastic bag. Although the surface of the kombu will appear chalky, do not rinse it. The powdery white substance is made up of natural glutamates that carry flavor (umami).

Miso

A staple of the Japanese kitchen, miso (fermented soybean paste) is most typically made by combining cooked soybeans with a grain (such as barley, wheat, rice, or millet) and a yeastlike mold and leaving the mixture to ferment for anywhere from several days to several years. It can be smooth or chunky, mild or robust flavored, and comes in a variety of colors, including white, red, beige, dark brown, and yellow. We use white miso (*shiro-miso*), which is delicately textured and flavored, in the recipes in this book.

Nori ⑦ ⑧

In the past, the Japanese word *nori* was translated as "laver," but nowadays nori is commonly understood by English speakers. A generic term for a variety of sea vegetables of the genus *Porphyra*, nori is most often sold in dried sheets, typically 8½ by 7½ in/

21.5 by 19 cm, in cellophane packages, with usually a dozen sheets to a pack **8**. You can buy the sheets cut to size for hand rolls **7**, as well. Nori also comes in toasted sheets (*yaki nori*) and in seasoned sheets (brushed with soy sauce and labeled *aji nori*). Once a package has been opened, store it in an airtight container away from sunlight and heat. Before using nori, always lightly toast it by passing it over an open flame on the stove top until it is crisp (see page 112). Toasting brings out its taste, texture, and fragrance. Untoasted nori is tough and lacks deep flavor. *Aonori*, dried powdered nori, is sold in cellophane bags or jars (sometimes labeled seaweed powder or flakes) and is used as a garnish in some sushi rolls and rice dishes. To release its full fragrance, rub it between your fingertips before using.

Rice, kome

The Japanese prefer short-grain white rice—plump kernels—for making sushi and other dishes. Almost all the Japanese-style short-grain rice sold in U.S. markets is grown in California, within 100 mi/161 km of Sacramento, the state capital.

Rice vinegar, komesu

About 350 years ago, in the Edo era, a sake brewer discovered how to brew vinegar by using sake lees (sediment left over from making sake) as the main ingredient. The amino acids and sugars in the lees produced a reddish vinegar with a unique flavor and sweetness. The vinegar, which was named *aka su* (red vinegar), helped popularize sushi-making in old Tokyo—rice was mixed with salt and the red vinegar, fresh fish pulled from Tokyo Bay were added, and sushi became the city's new fast food.

After World War II, vinegar makers in Japan lost the resources (i.e., rice) to make aka su, so most brewers switched to synthetic vinegar, and most sushi bars followed them, changing from aka su to clear synthetic rice vinegar.

Nowadays, vinegar makers are once again brewing authentic rice vinegar. Called *junmai su*, it is made from all-natural ingredients and is a light amber. It is the most common vinegar for sushi-making, because its deep flavor and mild sourness allow the taste of the rice to shine. Aka su is also being made today, and some sushi bars have returned to using it. It gives a slightly different taste to sushi than the more common rice vinegar does, as the sake lees impart a deeper flavor. Aka su is very difficult to find in markets in the United States, but if you have a Japanese market in your neighborhood, it is worth checking to see if it is available.

1 SAN-J TAMARI GLUTEN FREE SOY SAUCE · MADE WITH 100% SOY · NET 10 FL OZ (296 mL)

2 KIKKOMAN ALL-PURPOSE GLUTEN-FREE Soy Sauce · NATURALLY BREWED · 8.5 FL OZ (250mL)

4 S&B ORIENTAL HOT MUSTARD · NET WT. 3 OZ. (85 g)

7 TEMAKIYASAN 手巻やさん ファミリータイプ · Roasted Seaweed · 20 SHEETS (HALF CUT) · NET WEIGHT 0.88 oz. (25g) · BEST BEFORE 16OCT2013

3

5 S&B ICHIMI TOGARASHI · CHILI PEPPER · NET WT. 15g 0.52 OZ.

6 S&B さんしょうの粉

13

10 THE WHITE SHOYU · ヤマシン 白醤油 · ヤマシン株式会社

11 キッコーマン しょうゆ · kikkoman · ALL PURPOSE SEASONING

12 KIKKOMAN うすくち USUKUCHI LIGHT COLOR Soy Sauce · 33.8 FL OZ (1L) · OVER 300 YEARS OF EXCELLENCE

13 Nitrogen Flush for Freshness · SIGNATURE QUALITY · California Koshihikari Short Grain · カリフォルニア産コシヒカリ品種使用 · 限定契約農家直送 · 軽洗米 · 一選 · TAMAKI GOLD · 田牧米 · NEW CROP 新米 NEW CROP · NET WEIGHT 5LBS. 2.26 KG · TAMAKI RICE CORPORATION

8

9

14

15

Sake

Used in small amounts in sushi-making, sake, an alcoholic beverage made from fermented rice, is a natural tenderizer because of its amino acids. It also reduces saltiness and helps to eliminate fishy tastes and the strong odors of some ingredients. You do not need to use the same sake for sushi-making that you buy for drinking (see page 20). A lower-quality brand will work fine.

Salt

The recipes usually call for kosher salt and sometimes sea salt. Do not attempt to substitute table salt for kosher salt in the same amount. Table salt is much finer, so you need only half the amount specified for kosher salt. It is important to use sea salt whenever it is called for, as it imparts a different flavor than kosher or table salt.

Soy sauce, shōyu

This ubiquitous Japanese seasoning is traditionally made from soybeans, wheat (and sometimes rice), and salt. The beans are cooked, the wheat is toasted, and the two are then combined and inoculated with a mold that is allowed to grow for a few days. Next, the mixture is blended with a salt brine to make a mash, and the mash is left to ferment in a tank, typically for at least six months and sometimes longer. Finally, the mash is pressed to release the liquid and the liquid is refined, pasteurized, and bottled. Here are four soy sauces and a related term that you are likely to encounter as you explore the world of sushi.

Dark soy sauce, koikuchi shōyu

This soy sauce is most commonly found in sushi bars in the United States, where it is appreciated for its pleasant deep color and well-balanced taste. If a recipe calls simply for soy sauce, this is the type to use.

Gluten-free soy sauce

This soy sauce is usually made from soybeans, rice, water, and salt. Some brewers use a koji starter of steamed rice cultivated with a koji mold (the same starter that is used for sake). The wheat in regular soy sauce is replaced by rice.

Many brands are labeled as "tamari," but not all tamari are wheat-free. Tamari is a method for making soy sauce, so always read the label carefully.

Light soy sauce, usukuchi shōyu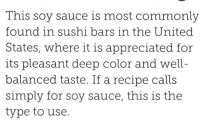

Made from the same ingredients as koikuchi shōyu, this soy sauce contains extra salt to halt fermentation sooner. It is dark amber (the term *light* in its name refers to its color, not its taste) and is clearer and thinner than dark soy sauce. But more important, it is saltier. Usukuchi shōyu is typically used when the deep color of koikuchi shōyu would darken the food too much.

White soy sauce, shiro shōyu

This sauce is made from steamed wheat, a smaller amount of toasted soybeans, salt, and yeast. (The ratio of soybeans to wheat for dark soy is reversed for white soy.) The amount of salt used is greater than what is used in usukuchi shōyu, which means the fermentation period is even shorter. This results in a soy sauce that is almost the color of pilsner beer, and it is generally used when you want the flavor of soy sauce but not the color.

Thick soy sauce, tamari

This soy sauce is usually darker and thicker than koikuchi shōyu. Most tamari is made from soybeans, salt, and yeast, but now some producers add about 1 percent toasted wheat to create a lighter fragrance. The wheat-free version is a good choice for anyone who suffers from gluten intolerance.

Murasaki

Murasaki means "purple" in Japanese, but it also means "soy sauce" at sushi bars in Japan, in reference to the color of the sauce. At good sushi bars, the chefs blend their own soy sauce, using different types of soy sauce and their own secret ingredients.

Sugar

We use regular granulated white cane sugar in our recipes.

Sushi vinegar, sushi-zu

The flavored vinegar used to make sushi rice contains rice vinegar, dashi kombu, sugar, and salt. Although sushi vinegar is easy to make (see page 111; if you are making sushi, the ingredients for it will already be in your pantry), and it is fresher and better when it is homemade, you can purchase already-made sushi vinegar at Japanese markets and some supermarkets.

Sweet rice wine, mirin

Made from steamed glutinous rice, shōchū, and koji (steamed rice treated with a specific mold), mirin (also known as *hon mirin*, or "true mirin") is a slightly syrupy cooking wine used to add a gentle sweetness and balance to dishes. After 40 to 60 days of slow fermentation, the glutinous rice starch and protein have decomposed and become sugars, amino acids, and organic acids, creating a unique sweet wine with an alcohol content of 8 to 14 percent, depending on the brand. If you cannot find mirin, do not sweeten sake as a substitute. Instead, use 1 tsp sugar for each 1 tbsp mirin. *Aji mirin*, a similar and less expensive product found in food stores and made from water, alcohol, salt, and sugar, is usually only about 1 percent alcohol, though some brands have a higher alcohol content. If you use it instead of hon mirin, you will need to reduce the salt in the recipe.

Wasabi 23

The word *wasabi* translates as "mountain hollyhock," and although wasabi is often compared to Western horseradish, the two roots are not members of the same genus. Wasabi, which is more fragrant and less sharp or hot than horseradish, is said to increase the appetite, promote digestion, and kill microbes. Unfortunately, true wasabi is hard to find, and most of the prepared "wasabi" available in sushi bars is Western white horseradish colored green, which also explains its nasal-clearing power. If you can find fresh wasabi, please use it. If not,

look for wasabi paste in a tube, which sometimes includes true wasabi along with horseradish. Pay a little more for a better-quality product. If you cannot find wasabi fresh or in a tube, look for powdered wasabi in small cans, which, despite the labeling, is usually just green-tinted horseradish. You mix the powder with water as directed on the can and then let the paste stand for about 10 minutes to develop the flavor.

If you do find fresh wasabi, to grate it, first trim out the "eyes" and pare away the tough brownish skin, exposing only as much of the flesh as you plan to grate. (Do not remove any leaves, as the root will keep better with the leaves intact.) Then, using a Japanese grater (see page 37), grate the flesh in a circular motion, creating a creamy, moist paste. Serve right away so the fragrant fresh flavor is not lost. To store the remainder of the root, stand it in a shallow plate of filtered or mineral water, cut-end down, or wrap in a moist paper towel and slip into a resealable plastic bag.

Condiments and Garnishes

Daikon

Many different varieties of daikon (also known as giant white radish or daikon radish) are grown in Japan. Some are long and slender and others are round and bulbous; some are sharp and spicy and others mild. Look for a long, slender root that has tight white skin, a fresh appearance (the stems and leaves should be pale green),

and feels heavy for its size. We prefer roots at least 12 in/30.5 cm long and about 2 in/5 cm in diameter and white from top to bottom. Pass up any daikon that is limp or soft. If you cannot find a daikon, an icicle radish can be substituted. Daikon is often used as a garnish, shredded or grated (see page 121), but it can also be braised and used as a topping for nigiri-zushi (see page 159).

Daikon sprouts, kaiware

These peppery, wispy sprouts, with their snow-white stems and small, dark green leaves, are sold in plastic cups with a growing medium in the bottom. You purchase the living sprouts and cut them from the container as you need them. They will keep in the package in the refrigerator for up to 1 week.

Dried chiles 5

The Japanese use a variety of small dried red chiles in various forms, including whole as well as flakes or threads. They are also ground into a coarse powder, which is used on its own or mixed with herbs and spices to make seven-spice pepper blend, or *shichimi tōgarashi* (see page 34).

Dried gourd strips, kampyō

To make these dried strips, a large pumpkinlike gourd (calabash or bottle gourd) is spiral cut to yield long, narrow ribbons, which are then either sun-dried or dehydrated by machine and sold in cellophane packages. Kampyō is typically used in sushi rolls or for tying a food package. Before use, the strips are softened by

kneading them with salt, rinsing them, and then boiling them in seasoned water until soft.

Fermented soybeans, natto

This ancient food product has such a distinctive flavor, smell, and texture that even half of the people in Japan don't like to eat it. Although it is a staple for breakfast and late-night snacks from Tokyo to the north, it is not eaten widely south of the city. It is made by treating soybeans with natto bacteria (a strain of *Bacillus subtilis*) and keeping the beans in a warm spot for a day. The beans are then cooled and aged for up to a week to develop their characteristic sticky stringiness. Sold in heavy plastic packets and tubes, great natto is now made in the United States, and you can find it in Japanese markets and some health-food markets.

Ginger 25

Ginger is a rhizome in the same family as turmeric, galangal, and cardamom. We prefer to find young ginger that has a thinner skin, which is light yellow to pink in color. Young ginger is less fibrous and not as pungent as older ginger. The easiest way to peel ginger is with a spoon. Only remove as much skin from the root as you need to, as the root keeps better with the skin on. Store ginger refrigerated in a resealable plastic bag for up to 2 months.

Green onion and chive

In Japan, cooks use *naganegi* (very long, thin green onions) as both a seasoning and a garnish.

They can be difficult to find in U.S. markets, however, where they are typically labeled Japanese leeks. Green onions can be substituted. Regular chives and garlic chives are used in sushi-making, usually as a garnish and occasionally as a tie on a nigiri-zushi.

Japanese cucumber, kyūri

Nearly seedless and with crisp, flavorful flesh, Japanese cucumbers are at their best when they are about 8 in/20 cm long and ¾ to 1 in/2 to 2.5 cm in diameter. If you have a vegetable garden, they are easy to grow. If you don't, look for them in Japanese markets and some farmers' markets. You can also use an English cucumber in place of the Japanese cucumber, removing any errant seeds first and peeling the skin if tough.

Japanese ginger, myōga

A relative of ginger, *myōga*, which is prized for its shoots and buds, has a taste reminiscent of its kin, thus its English name. In the past, it was foraged in woodlands, but now it is cultivated and available year-round. The bud, which is a deep rose with green tips, is usually finely shredded or diced and used as a garnish, and the shoots are eaten as a vegetable. Myōga will keep in a closed plastic bag in the refrigerator for up to 1 week.

Japanese mustard, karashi

Deep yellow Japanese mustard frequently has wasabi or horseradish mixed into it to make it spicy-hot. It is sold in tubes and in powder form, which is reconstituted with water.

Japanese pepper, sanshō

The seedpods of the prickly ash tree, sometimes called the Japanese pepper tree (which is related to the Szechwan pepper), are known as sanshō, or Japanese pepper. Unlike those of a true pepper tree, the seeds are never used. Instead, the pods are split open, the seeds are discarded, and the pods are dried and ground to a powder called *kona sanshō*. The ground pods have a flavor reminiscent of pepper but with more fragrance and no heat. Sanshō is used mainly with fatty grilled foods, such as eel and chicken, to mask the taste of the fat. If you've ever experienced a tingling numbness in your mouth during a Japanese meal, it's due to the addition of some form of sanshō in the dish. The young fresh leaves are known as *kinome* and have a bright floral fragrance, a slight medicinal note, and a touch of mint flavor. They are available in the spring and can be used as a garnish and in sauces.

Kanzuri

A specialty of the mountainous Niigata region, on the island of Honshu, this prized spicy paste is made from chiles that are harvested, salted, and then left in the snow to ferment. The fermented chiles are mixed with rice malt, yuzu, and other ingredients and aged for three years to form a spicy paste with a floral, fragrant aroma. It is sold in small jars in Japanese and other Asian markets.

Lemon

The Eureka lemon can be used for most of the recipes in this book. Occasionally, when we prefer a more floral, sweeter note, we like to use Meyer lemons.

Lime

The Bearss lime, the variety most commonly sold in supermarkets, can be used for the recipes in this book. If Key limes, also known as Mexican limes, are available, they will impart a more fragrant flavor with a bit more acid.

Mountain Yam, Naga-imo and Yama-imo 18

There are two varieties of yams that the Japanese refer to as "long potato" or "mountain yam." True to their name, these are very long tubers, ranging from 2 to 3.5 in/5 to 9 cm in diameter and can be up to 2 ft/ 61 cm long. They have a rough, hairy, beige to dark brown skin.

In most Asian markets, mountain potatoes are sold in 7-in/17-cm manageable pieces, packed in sawdust to keep moisture at bay. To use, first peel; their texture is a bit slimy but crunchy, and the flavor is very mild. They are usu-ally grated and added to noodle dishes or *okonomiyaki* (Japanese pancake), or cut into sticks and served with pickled plum, which is very refreshing. It is a good idea to wear gloves while prepping, since the flesh, when peeled, can irritate sensitive skin.

Pickled ginger, gari 20

To make *gari*, young, tender ginger is thinly sliced and lightly pickled in a mixture of vinegar, salt, and sugar (see page 120). A slice or two of gari is eaten between bites of sushi to cleanse the palate. It is also sometimes used as a garnish on nigiri-zushi or sushi bowls.

Pickled plum, uméboshi 24

Umé are pickled small unripe "plums" (they are actually a species of apricot). They are cured in salt for at least three months, usually with red shiso leaves that impart a wonderful flavor and color, though many people keep them much longer. Dried bonito flakes (kezuri-bushi) are sometimes added to the plums along with the shiso, so check the ingredients carefully if you want to ensure you have a vegetarian condiment. Uméboshi are typically sold in clear plastic containers in Japa-nese and other Asian markets. It is believed that eating the pickled plums aids digestion and helps to keep the intestinal tract clear, which is one reason why they are almost always served as part of a Japanese breakfast.

Quail egg

About 1 in/2.5 cm long, these tasty eggs have ivory or white shells marked with brown speckles. Look for the eggs in Japanese markets and some specialty stores. The yolk is a popular ingredient in gunkan-maki (see pages 174 and 177), where it is used raw. (Although the incidence of salmonella in eggs is very low, diners who have a compromised immune system, are pregnant, are older, or are young children should avoid foods that include raw eggs.)

Sesame seeds, goma

Two types of sesame seeds are used in the Japanese kitchen: white (*shiro goma*) and black (*kuro goma*). White sesame seeds, which are generally lightly toasted, are more common in sushi-making than black sesame seeds, which are not toasted. Although you can buy toasted (or roasted) sesame seeds, it is best to toast them yourself, as they will be more fragrant and a fresher product. To toast them, place them in a dry, heavy skillet over medium heat and heat, swirling the pan or stirring the seeds with a wooden spatula to prevent overbrowning, just until the seeds begin to color and are fragrant, about 1 minute, then immediately pour them out onto a plate. Also, make sure that you purchase your seeds in a shop with high turn-over. Old seeds can turn rancid and impart an off flavor. Store the seeds in an airtight container in the refrigerator or freezer.

Seven-spice pepper blend, shichimi tōgarashi

This blend varies depending on the packager, though it always includes seven ingredients. A common mix would be chile, sesame seeds, ginger, citrus peel, flaxseed or hemp seeds, sanshō, and nori.

Shiso, perilla, beefsteak plant 16

A relative of mint and easily cul-tivated, shiso is available in two types, *aojiso* (green shiso) and *akajiso* (red shiso). Green shiso leaves are used as a garnish, in sushi rolls, and also as a tempura vegetable. The flavor of the dark green sawtooth leaves is often described as a cross between mint and basil, and, in a pinch, you could substitute a mixture of those. Red shiso leaves are used primarily for pickling and in some sweets. Its tiny sprouts (*mejiso*) and the tiny buds of its flowering seedpods (*hanajiso*; the regular seedpods are called *hojiso*) are used for garnishing sashimi, or you can add the seedpods to the soy sauce in your dipping bowl.

Spicy grated daikon, momiji oroshi

This mildly spicy condiment, which accompanies both sushi and sashimi, is a mixture of grated daikon and pepper. Although it can be purchased in jars in Japanese and other Asian markets, it is also easy to make at home (see page 121).

Yuzu

A type of citrus, yuzu resembles a lemon or lime, depending on its age, and is about the size of a tangerine. In some sources, it is called a Japanese citron, but because it is usually identified as *yuzu* in food stores, we are using that term throughout the book. Although a number of different varieties exist, they are all labeled simply *yuzu* and any type you use will be fine. The fruit is primarily appreciated for its peel, though some varieties have enough juice to extract and use for seasoning. The fruit has grown in popularity in the last decade or so, and the juice is easier to find bottled. It is still difficult to find the fresh fruit, however, which is both seasonal and expensive. If you buy the

juice, be sure to buy a brand that requires refrigeration. It will be more costly, but it will also contain fewer additives.

Sudachi

The highly fragrant *sudachi*, another common Japanese citrus fruit that is smaller than the yuzu and has bumpier skin, can be used in place of yuzu. The fruits are harvested for cooking when they are green. If left on the tree, they will turn yellow and eventually orange.

Yuzu with pepper, yuzu koshō

This condiment is made by grinding yuzu peel and salt to a paste and then adding either hot green chile, which yields a green paste, or hot red chile, which yields a red paste. It is sold in small jars in Japanese markets. Use it sparingly, as it is very spicy and pungent.

Tools and Equipment

Bamboo sushi mat 28

Also known as a sushi mat or *sudaré*, this flat, flexible mat, typically about 10 in/25 cm square, is made of strips of bamboo woven together with cotton string. Its primary use is for making rolled sushi, but it also can be used to squeeze out excess moisture from cooked leafy vegetables or to let a *tamago* (egg) roll drain. The bamboo strips can be thick or thin. The mats with thicker strips are easier to use, but the mats with thinner ones are necessary for rolling the skinny rolls known as *hosomaki*.

Chopsticks

Kitchen chopsticks are not like eating chopsticks. First, they are longer, typically starting at about 12 in/30.5 cm. They are made of wood or bamboo and are usually joined at the top by a piece of string. If keeping them attached bothers you, you can remove the string. Once you get used to kitchen chopsticks, you will find them indispensable. They are handy for stirring or beating, for grasping a single piece of food in a pot of boiling water or hot oil, for turning and poking all kinds of hot foods on the stove top, and for arranging foods on a plate.

Cutting board 42

The type of cutting board you use is a personal choice; wood, plastic composite, and bamboo are the most common materials. The board should be big enough to fit over your sink, so that when you are breaking down a fish, you can run water on the cutting board at the same time to keep the mess under control. It is helpful to have a second, slightly smaller board for your worktable. After each use, clean the cutting boards well, using hot, soapy water (if using wooden boards, the water should be only slightly soapy, as too much soap will dry out the wood), and let them drain to prevent bacterial growth.

Deep-frying equipment

For deep-frying, you need a deep, heavy pot, preferably cast iron. You can find decent deep fryers on the market nowadays, but many do not hold a temperature well or do not get hot enough, even though the gauge says they

do, so a regular pot is better. The pot must be deep because the oil must be deep enough to immerse the foods completely, and the pot must be no more than half full of oil. As you add ingredients to the hot oil, the oil will rise and bubble up and can boil over, so the depth of the pot is critical.

You will also need a good-quality digital deep-frying thermometer that you can clip on to the rim of the pot. This allows you to check the temperature regularly and to make sure the oil returns to the correct temperature before each new batch of food is added. A net ladle—a flat, round, long-handled fine-mesh strainer about 5 in/12 cm in diameter—is handy for lifting out some foods from the hot oil and for removing little bits of batter or other ingredients that accumulate in the oil and can burn. Finally, you will need kitchen chopsticks (see page 35) or tongs and a sheet pan or other surface lined with paper towels or topped with a wire rack for draining deep-fried foods.

Donburi

Literally "bowl," donburi is the name for both the vessel itself and the rice dish that is served in it. The bowls, which areused for individual servings of chirashi-zushi and other one-bowl rice dishes, typically measure 6 to 8 in/ 15 to 20 cm in diameter and about 4 in/10 cm deep. They are versatile additions to any kitchen.

Fan, *uchiwa*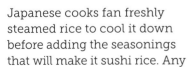

Japanese cooks fan freshly steamed rice to cool it down before adding the seasonings that will make it sushi rice. Any type of handheld fan will work for this task. If you use a folding fan and it has a lock that keeps it open, you will have one less thing to distract you as you fan.

Fish scaler 35

Fish scalers come in many shapes and sizes. In general, the simpler the style, the easier the scaler is to use. A good model is sturdy but not sharp, does not bend when you are working with it, and its teeth will not dig into the flesh of the fish. Choose a scaler that fits your hand and feels comfortable when you grip it tightly.

Fish tweezers 34

These look like oversize eyebrow tweezers but are heavier and made from stronger metal. They make it easy to remove pin bones from fish without tearing the flesh. Look for a stainless-steel pair that fits your hand well, is easy to grasp and maneuver, and has even, blunt ends.

Graters 32 33

We use two types of Japanese graters. The first, more traditional grater is made of stainless steel, tin, or ceramic and is used for grating wasabi, daikon, and ginger 33. (There is also a small sharkskin grater designed specifically for preparing wasabi; see page 31. It is neither big nor expensive and ensures a very good paste.) It has a flat surface with raised spikes and a trough at one end, and it looks like a shovel head with thornlike points. The second grater is a bit easier to use. Made of ceramic, it is a round, shallow bowl shape with a raised grating area in the center

and often a silicone seal on the bottom to keep it from sliding as you grate 32. A small, soft bamboo brush is handy for removing the gratings from both styles, saving your fingers.

Grill

You have several choices here. You can use a big outside grill, a small hibachi, a small tabletop grill, a grill pan, or a grill screen. Of these possibilities, the one that most U.S. cooks are unfamiliar with is the grill screen. Handy because it offers an easy way to grill indoors, it is a flat, thin grid that you put directly over a gas flame on the stove top. They are also used for small items that would fall through the grates of a regular grill rack.

Kitchen torch

A butane kitchen torch, available at most cookware stores (or an all-purpose propane torch, good for plumbing and cooking), is handy for searing a bonito fillet for *tataki* (a traditional technique; see page 78), charring vegetables for topping sushi, and other uses.

Knives 36 – 41

We recommend that you have three basic knives. The first is a traditional chef's knife 39 with a medium-thick blade and a length of between 6 and 8 in/ 15 and 20 cm (excluding the handle). It is good for cutting through hard bones and filleting. The Japanese knife for the same purpose is called a *deba-bōchō* 36, usually shorter than a Western-style chef's knife and thicker. There are left-handed and right-handed versions.

The second knife **40**, used for slicing, has a blade that is at least 8 in/20 cm long, about 1¼ in/3 cm wide, and 1⁄16 to 1⁄8 in/2 to 3 mm thick. Ideal for cutting a slice from a fish fillet in a single stroke, the Japanese knife for this purpose may be labeled *yanagi-bōchō* or *sashimi-bōchō* **37**. Left-handed and right-handed versions are available.

The third knife **38** **41**, with a blade about 4 in/10 cm long, is a small utility knife used for prepping vegetables and filleting small whole fish.

Omelet pan **31**

This is a specialty item, and although not a necessity, it is a beautiful object to own and is the best pan to use for making a Japanese omelet. Known as a *dashi-maki tamago* pan, it is rectangular and typically measures about 5 in/12 cm wide, 7 in/17 cm long, and 1 in/2.5 cm deep. The pans are made of cast iron, heavy aluminum, or, the best, tin coated with copper. If you buy a pan, use it only for making Japanese omelets to ensure the finish lasts.

Rice cooker

Many different types of rice cookers are available today, from ones to which you just add rice and water and push a button to those that can also be used to cook all kinds of rice dishes. Some use fuzzy logic to cook rice based on moisture and the amount of water added. It is not necessary to buy the most expensive rice cooker, but you should get one that makes a minimum of 8 cups/1.3 kg cooked rice.

Wooden rice bowl **27**

Known as a *hangiri*, this beautiful shallow bowl (about 5 in/12 cm deep) is traditionally made of cedar and banded with copper. It comes in different diameters, from about 12 in/30.5 cm to about 18 in/46 cm. If you have the choice, select the larger size. When making sushi rice, spread the cooked rice in the bowl and then mix in the vinegar while fanning at the same time. The bowl should be wide enough so that the layer of rice is not too thick but still thick enough to cut through with a wooden rice paddle (see following entry).

Wooden rice paddle **30**

Known as a *shamoji*, this paddle, which is traditionally made of wood or bamboo, is used to turn the rice when you are cooling it and mixing in the vinegar. To prevent the rice from sticking to the paddle, always dampen the paddle well with water before using. Use the paddle only for making sushi rice, as wood and bamboo are porous and will take on flavors from other foods and pass them along to the rice.

Sushi
Basics

In this chapter, you will find instructions for how to break down various types of fish and shell-fish for sushi, along with recipes for curing mack-erel; for making dashi, a dashi-flavored rolled omelet, sushi rice, and a variety of sushi gar-nishes and condiments; and other basics. In the following three chapters, you will learn how to put these basic techniques and recipes to work making sushi.

We begin with detailed instructions for breaking down several types of fish and shellfish. When shopping for them, always ask the fishmonger when the fish or shellfish came in. If you do not like the answer, ask to see what did come in that day. When selecting a whole fresh fish, look for shiny skin, clear eyes, and bright red gills. Smell the fish, too. It should have a sweet ocean smell. If the skin has dry patches, the eyes look cloudy, the gills are a dull red, or you detect a fishy odor, look for another fish.

Identifying good-quality shellfish varies accord-ing to type. For example, squid should have shiny white skin and clear eyes. If the body has a pinkish tone, the squid is not fresh enough for sushi. A lobster should move about when lifted, eels should look shiny and moist, and cherry-stone or other small clams should close to the touch and feel heavy for their size. When you are buying clams, always toss in a couple of extra ones. Because you cannot see inside their shells, you cannot be sure of the quality, and it is wise to have some backup.

How to
Break Down Flatfish

California halibut and flounder (hirame), fluke (karei), sand dab, sole (shitabirame)

All flatfish have one thing in common: both eyes are on the same side of their head. They live on the ocean floor, and because their bodies are very thin and the side that faces away from the seabed is usually colored to prevent detection (this is also the side with the eyes), they move about the water unseen by predators but able to see around them. Their flesh is typically very mild and low in fat, and their bones are great for stock. For sushi preparation, we prefer flatfish that weigh from 1 to 6 lb/455 g to 2.75 kg.

Scale the fish

First, rinse the fish well under cold running water. Place the fish in a plastic bag large enough to give you room to maneuver your hands easily. The bag will help contain the flying scales, keeping any mess to a minimum. Using a fish scaler and working on one side of the fish, scrape the scales from the tail toward the head (against the direction the scales grow) to remove them. Repeat on the other side of the fish. Rinse the fish under cold running water, then check to make sure no scales remain by running your hands along the fish from the tail to the head. If you have a sink large enough for the fish to lie flat, you can dispense with the bag and scale the fish in the sink. Allow a small stream of cool tap water to run over the fish as you work, to keep the scales in the sink.

Identify the anatomy of the fish

Place the fish on a cutting board with the head to the left and the tail to the right and with the darker skin–side up and whiter-side down. (If you are left-handed, reverse the direction of the head of the fish here and equivalent directions elsewhere, and use your left hand to wield the knife throughout the instructions.) To identify the extent of the head, which will be removed first, move your finger from the middle of the body toward the head. There will be a change in the firmness as you reach the head. The head will be solid and hard. Before the head can be removed, the belly needs to be identified to ensure you don't damage the entrails, which can have a strong odor and/or are extremely bitter and can contaminate the flesh. The location of the belly depends on the type of flatfish. One way to determine the location of the belly is by its relationship to the mouth. The mouth is just next to the eyes, and the belly is on the same side as the mouth. Another method of detecting the location of the belly is to press along the body of the fish with your fingertips. Half of the body will feel softer to the touch. The softer side is where the belly is located.

Cut off the head and remove the entrails

Holding the head firmly with your left hand (use a kitchen towel, if necessary, to prevent slippage), and following the outline of the head you have identified, cut off the head with a chef's knife (1). The head can be saved for making stock. By cutting off the head, you have exposed the cavity where the entrails of the flatfish are housed. Under running cold water, grasp and remove the entrails. If there is roe, do not remove it at this time. The entrails should come out easily. Work carefully to avoid damaging them and

Break Down Flatfish

contaminating the flesh. Use a small spoon to scrape out as much of the blood line as possible. Then, rinse the outside and the cavity of the fish under cold running water and scrub the cavity gently with a small brush, like a toothbrush. If you find roe in the cavity, see page 52 for how to prepare it.

Fillet the fish
Clean and dry the cutting board well. Pat the fish dry with paper towels. Line a sheet pan with parchment paper. Place the fish back on the cutting board, darker skin–side up and whiter-side down, the head side to the left and the tail to the right, and cut off the tail (2, 3). Turn the fish so the head side is away from you and the tail end is close to the front edge of the board. Running lengthwise down the middle of the fish is a line of dark dots. This marks the location of the backbone under the flesh. Using the

chef's knife, insert the blade at the top of the head end where the dark dots start. The knife should touch the backbone. Now, keeping the tip of the knife in contact with the backbone, start the cut and follow the line of dark dots from the head end to the end of the tail (4).

Locate the top, or peak, of the backbone with your fingertip. Starting at the head end, slide your knife into the peak at a 45-degree angle, with the blade facing left. Run the knife in a shallow cut along the side of the backbone and just touching the spines that extend almost parallel to the cutting board. Make the cut the whole length of the fish. The next cut starts at the tail end (5), but flatten the angle of the knife slightly so that the blade is against the backbone and then carefully cut along the spines all the way to the head end. If the fish is small, this second cut may be

sufficient to remove the whole fillet. If the fish is large, you will need to make one or two more cuts to remove the fillet (6). The important thing is to keep the knife angled against the spines so that none of the flesh is left behind. Once the fillet is removed, place it on the prepared sheet pan (7), cover with plastic wrap, and refrigerate.

Turn the fish around on the cutting board so the tail end is away from you and the head end is close to the front edge of the board. Starting at the tail end (8) and cutting toward the head end (9), repeat the process to remove the fillet on the second side (10), then refrigerate the second fillet with the first fillet. To remove the fillets from the opposite side of the fish, turn the fish over and position it with the head end away from you and the tail end at the front edge of the board closest to you. Repeat the process to remove the remaining two fillets and refrigerate them along with the others. Reserve the bones and head to make Nigiri with California Halibut Aspic (hirame no nikogori; page 136). Or, if you don't plan on making nikogori, you can make stock or freeze the head and bones to make stock when you have time.

Remove the small bones and skin

The skin of the fish protects the flesh from oxidation, so it is best not to remove it until just before you are ready to use the fish. Place a fillet, skin-side down, vertically on the cutting board, with the thicker side of the fillet to your left. Run you finger along the edge of the thicker side of the fillet. If you feel any small bones, slice straight down to remove them (11), removing as little flesh as possible (12). Place your finger alongside the fin muscle (13) to identify where to separate. Slice off the fin muscle, separating it from the fillet (14,15). This muscle, called *engawa* in Japanese, has an interesting texture and fatty flavor. Move the fillet parallel to the front edge of the board, with the tail end to your left. Hold the very edge of the tail end down firmly with the index finger of your left hand, place the knife tip directly next to your fingertip, and slice down to the skin (16). When the blade reaches the skin, using a small sawing motion, gradually change the angle of the knife so that the blade is flat and pointed to the right. Now, begin cutting toward the right between the flesh and the skin. Once enough skin is exposed to grasp, hold the skin firmly with your left hand (17), keeping it taut by pulling to the left. Use a little downward force on the knife while you move the skin in a back-and-forth motion and pull it to the left. Eventually the movement of the skin will start the cut. The knife is not doing the work; the cut is made by the movement of the skin (18). Once the fillet is freed, refrigerate and repeat the process on the other three fillets.

How to

Break Down Flatfish

1

2

>>>

5

6

3

4

7

8

How to

Break Down Flatfish

9

10

>>>

13

14

11

12

15

16

How to
Break Down Flatfish

17

18

How to
Slice Flatfish Fillet for Nigiri

These directions are for when you buy a fillet from a fishmonger, or after breaking down a whole fish. The majority of the nigiri recipes in this book require slices of fish that are about 3 in/7.5 cm long, 1 in/2.5 cm wide, and ¼ in/6 mm thick. But use your best judgment when it comes to how thick your cuts should be. This will depend on the type of fish, its size, and the tenderness of its flesh. For example, if the fish is chewy, cut it a bit thinner. If your fish is very tender, use our suggested thickness, or even slice it slightly thicker.

Trim the fillet to the size for nigiri
Examine the fillet you just broke down or purchased. If you started with a whole fish the size we suggested, you will have roughly ¾-in-/2-cm-thick cuts from the upper fillets, and ½-in-/12-mm-thick cuts from the bottom fillets. The width at the widest point will be about 2 in/5 cm after you've removed the fin muscles (*engawa*). The width should be perfect to make 3-in/7.5-cm slices at an angle.

Remove the skin (see page 45) just before you start slicing the fillet for nigiri.

If the fillet is thicker than 1¼ in/ 3 cm, place it skinned-side down on a cutting board. Using a slicing knife, and keeping the blade angle parallel to the cutting board, trim off the top of the fillet horizontally from the right end to get the thickness of the bottom part of

the fillet close to 1 in/2.5 cm. If the piece is close to 2 in/5 cm, cut in half horizontally.

If the fillet you have is wider than 3 in/7.5 cm, it needs to be trimmed closer to 3 in/7.5 cm. Look at the belly flap of the fillet; if the flap end is very thin, you need to trim off the part that is thinner to at least ⅛ in/3 mm thick. The trimmings can be chopped and used for gunkan-maki or donburi.

Slice the trimmed fillet for nigiri
Place one of the fillets on the cutting board, skin-side down. The basic idea is that you want to slice from the thicker end (this was the head end) of the fillet against the sinew, which runs from the head to the tail. Place the thicker side to the left on the cutting board, hold the left end with your left-hand

index and middle fingers, and make slices from the left end. But consider the following before you start slicing:

You need to imagine what each fillet will yield. Visualize the knife angle you need to slice the suggested piece of fish for nigiri. You may place your slicing knife above the fillet and move it around to get the idea of the best angle to get a slice closest to 3 in/7.5 cm long. Once you get the angle right, then look at the fillet from the front to see the second angle of the knife to make about 1-in-/2.5-cm-wide slices. Once you have both angles in your mind, position the fillet appropriately on the cutting board so you can make the slice comfortably.

When making the initial cut, consider whether the end of the fish is flat or uneven. If it is uneven, the initial cut can be as thick as necessary to make a flat, even

How to
Slice Flatfish Fillet for Nigiri

side to slice from. Make the initial cut using the slicing knife, using the full length of the blade from the heel to the tip in one motion (19, 20). As you go, adjust the angles of the knife blade to achieve the same-size slices. The tail end usually has more sinew; if it's too chewy, chop it for gunkan-maki or donburi.

For a thick fillet
If the fillet is trimmed to about 1 in/2.5 cm thick or a little thicker, place the fillet on the cutting board. You will slice from the right end. Again you can move your slicing knife above the fillet to adjust the angle so you can make 3-in-/7.5-cm-long slices, but this time you don't need to adjust the second angle because your fillet is already about 1 in/2.5 cm thick.

Holding the fillet near the right end with your left-hand index and middle fingers, make an initial cut straight down using the slicing knife, using the full length of the

blade from the heel to the tip in one motion. When making the initial cut, consider whether the end of the fish is flat or uneven. If it is uneven, the initial cut can be as thick as necessary to make a flat, even side to slice from. As you go, with each slice you make (21) you will need to adjust the angle of the knife to achieve the same 3-in-/7.5-cm-long slices. When you reach the thinner part of the fillet, you will need to make the slices at an angle to achieve 1-in-/2.5-cm-wide slices. This time you need to turn the fillet so that the thicker side is to the left and the thin side is to the right. Continue to make slices from the left end.

A Note about Flatfish Roe

When you remove the entrails from a flatfish, you may be lucky enough to find eggs, or roe (as you see in photographs 4 through 10 on pages 46 to 48). Look deep inside of the fish. The roe will be enclosed in a light beige-to-orange sac with a little veining on it. If you see the sac at this point, do not try to remove it, as it will likely break and the roe will become unusable. Once you have removed the first belly-side fillet from the fish, you will be able to see the entire roe sac. Gently lift it out, rinse it in a bowl of cold water, and then refrigerate it immediately.

To prepare the roe, in a saucepan, make a dashi mixture by combining 8 parts dashi (page 114), 1 part soy sauce, 1 part mirin, and a pinch of peeled and grated fresh ginger. Bring the mixture to a simmer, add the roe sac, and cook gently until the sac is slightly firm, 3 to 5 minutes, depending on the size of the roe sac. Remove from the heat, transfer the roe sac and cooking liquid to a heat-proof bowl, let cool, cover, and refrigerate until well chilled.

To serve the roe, remove the roe sac from the liquid, pat dry, and slice into disks 1/4 in/6 mm thick. Place a disk of roe on a piece of flatfish nigiri and garnish with chopped chives. The addition of the roe will give depth and texture to your nigiri-zushi.

19

20

21

How to

Break Down Round Fish

amberjack (*kanpachi*), arctic char (*hokkyoku iwana*), black cod (*gindara*), kingfish (*hiramasa*), salmon (*sake*), true snapper (*madai*), sea bass (*suzuki*), ocean trout (*umi-masu*)

Round fish, which are grouped together because they share a similar bone structure, are the most common fish used for sushi. Their similarities end there, however. They each have their own flavor, texture, and size. Learning how to break down this group of fish will be helpful in preparing dishes other than sushi, too. For example, if you wanted to grill a whole fish, because you will know the bone structure, you will be the master of filleting and serving it at the table.

Scale the fish

First, rinse the fish well under cold running water. Place the fish in a plastic bag large enough to give you room to maneuver your hands easily. The bag will help contain the flying scales, keeping any mess to a minimum. Using a fish scaler and working on one side of the fish, scrape the scales from the tail toward the head (1) (against the direction the scales grow) to remove them. Repeat on the other side of the fish. Make sure you remove the scales near the fins. The area has many small scales, and you need to remove them all before you make a cut. Rinse the fish under cold running water, then check to make sure no scales remain by running your hands along the fish from the tail to the head. If you have a sink large enough for the fish to lie flat, you can dispense with the bag and scale the fish in the sink. Allow a small stream of cool tap water to run over the fish as you work, to keep the scales in the sink.

Cut off the head and remove the entrails

Place the fish on the cutting board with the head to the left and the belly facing you. (If you are left-handed, reverse the direction of the head of the fish here and equivalent directions elsewhere, and use your left hand to wield the knife throughout the instructions.) There are three points on the fish that form a line to guide you in cutting off the head. To locate the first one, run your finger along the top side of the head toward the dorsal fin. Where you feel a change from hard bone to firm flesh, you have reached the first point. A second point is just to the right side of the pectoral fin, and the last point is just to the right side of the pelvic fin. Grab the head firmly with your left hand (if it is slippery or sharp, grip it with a kitchen towel) and place a chef's knife at a 45-degree angle toward the head of the fish. Starting the cut at the right side of the head (2), slice along the right side of the gill cover and pectoral fin and end just right of the pelvic fin, slicing down to the backbone. When the knife hits the backbone, change the angle of the knife to straight down and cut though the backbone but not through the fish. Turn the fish over so that the head is to the left and the dorsal fin is facing you. Using the knife at the same 45-degree angle to start (3), repeat the procedure in reverse, this time cutting off the head. Work carefully to avoid damaging the entrails. Some entrails have a strong odor and/or are extremely bitter and can contaminate the flesh. Remove the gills and save the head for making stock, if desired.

Turn the fish over so the belly is facing you. Starting at the anus, insert the tip of the knife into the fish and draw the knife up to the head end, cutting open the belly. Remove and discard the entrails. Rinse the cavity with cold running water.

Clean and dry the cutting board well. Place the fish back on the cutting board, with the tail to the left and the belly facing you. Although the entrails have been pulled out, some additional attached parts may still need to be removed, especially if the fish is in the bass family or the snapper family. Hold the body with the four fingers of your left hand and open the belly flap with your left thumb. You will see a puffy white sac where the rib cage meets the backbone (4). This is the swim bladder. On some fish, it will have come out when you removed the entrails. If it did not, you need to cut through the bladder to remove the blood line.

Cut open the bladder from the right to the left. Inside the bladder, make two cuts along the top and the bottom of the backbone the full length of the bladder (5). This will expose the back of the bladder, which will reveal the dark red line behind it. This is the blood line. Use a small spoon to scrape out as much of the blood line as possible. Then, rinse the outside and the cavity of the fish under cold running water and scrub the cavity gently with a small brush, like a toothbrush (6).

Fillet the fish
Clean and dry the cutting board well. Pat the fish dry with paper towels. Line a sheet pan with parchment paper. Place the fish back on the cutting board with the tail side to the left and close to the front end of the cutting board, the head side to the right and slightly away from the front edge of the cutting board, and the belly facing you. Place the

four fingers of your left hand on the body and gently press down on the back side so the stomach rises up (it is easier to see the inside of the cavity at this angle). Keep the initial cut shallow so that you know where the spines are. Starting at the anus, make a shallow cut through the skin toward the tail, going through just above the anal fin (7). You should feel the spines underneath the knife blade. Stay as close to the spines as possible to waste less flesh by leaving it on the bone. Use your left thumb to lift and open the front end of the top fillet. Place the knife at the same entry point and make a deeper cut, sliding the knife all the way along the backbone.

Turn the fish clockwise, moving the head side to the left and close to the front of the cutting board, the tail to the right and slightly away from you, and the dorsal fin facing you. Press the stomach side of the body to lift

Break Down Round Fish

up the back side. Keep the initial cut shallow so that you know where the spines are. Place the knife at the tail and along the soft dorsal fin and cut toward the head end, staying just above the spiny dorsal fin and ending at the head end (8). You should feel the spines underneath the knife blade as you work. Use your left thumb to lift and open the front of the top fillet, then slice open from the tail to the head side along the backbone.

Using the thumb and index finger of your left hand on either side, lift the fillet right next to the tail and pinch slightly. Slide the tip of your knife under the fillet, with the blade tip facing the tail. Disconnect the fillet from the backbone toward the tail without disconnecting the tail (9). Remove the knife from the fish, turn the knife to face the head end, and insert the knife in the same location but with the tip 1 in/2.5 cm past the backbone. Hold the tail firmly with your left hand, using a

kitchen towel if necessary to make it more secure. Holding the blade with a slightly downward angle along the backbone and using full force, slide the knife toward the head side to cut through and disconnect the rib-cage bones from the backbone (10). Place the knife back where the initial cut started and complete the removal of the fillet by cutting toward the tail along the backbone (11). Place the upper fillet on the prepared sheet pan, cover with plastic wrap, and refrigerate.

Turn the half-filleted fish (12) over. The backbone is now on the cutting board. Turn the fish clock-wise, moving the tail to the left and close to the front of the cutting board, the head end to the right and slightly away from you, and the dorsal fin facing you. Gently hold the fish with the four fingers of your left hand. Keep the initial cut shallow so that you know where the spines are. Place the knife just above the spiny dorsal

fin and make a shallow cut to open the fish from the head end, staying just above the soft dor-sal fin, all the way to the tail (13). Feel the spines underneath your knife blade as you work. Use your left thumb to lift and open the front end of the fillet, then slice open from the head end to the tail along the backbone. Do not release the tail.

Turn the fish so the head side is to the left and close to the front end of the cutting board, the tail is to the right and slightly away, and the belly is to the front. Gently hold the fish with the four fingers of your left hand. Keep the initial cut shallow so that you know where the spines are. Insert the knife at the tail and make a shallow cut through the skin toward the anal fin. Cut through just above the anal fin (14). You should feel the spines underneath the knife blade as you work. Stay as close to the spines as possible to waste less flesh by leaving it on the bone.

Use your left thumb to lift and open the front end of the fillet (15). Place the knife at the same entry point and make a deeper cut, sliding the knife all the way along the backbone.

Using the thumb and index finger of your left hand on either side, lift the fillet right next to the tail and pinch slightly. Slide the tip of your knife under the fillet, with the blade tip facing the tail (16). Disconnect the fillet from the backbone toward the tail without disconnecting the tail. Remove the knife from the fish, turn the knife to face the head end, and insert in the same location but with the knife tip 1 in/2.5 cm past the backbone. Hold the tail firmly with your left hand, using a kitchen towel if necessary to make it more secure. Holding the blade at a slightly downward angle, slide the knife along the backbone toward the head end until you feel the resistance of the rib cage against the blade. Place

your left hand at the head end and lift the belly flap with your left thumb. Continue the cut toward the head, disconnecting the rib cage from the backbone. Cut the tail free from the body (17).

Remove the rib cage
Place the fillet on the cutting board with the skin-side down, the head side to the left and slightly away from you, and the tail to the right and close to the front of the board. Hold the upper-left side of the fillet stable with the four fingers of your left hand. Place the tip of the knife, with the tip facing up, under where the first rib-cage bone meets the pin bones (about the middle of the fillet) (18). Cut and disconnect the rib-cage bone from the pin bones, then slide the knife to the next juncture of rib-cage bone and pin bones and cut and disconnect. Repeat until all the pin bones are disconnected.

Turn the fillet so the head end is to the right and close to the front

edge of the cutting board and the belly is facing you. Hold the rib cage with the four fingers of your left hand and place the knife under the rib cage at the point where you just disconnected the pin bones. Keeping the knife against the rib cage, slice it off (19).

Remove the pin bones
Place the fillet on the cutting board with the skin-side down and the tail end to the left. Put a small bowl of water on the right end (or left end if you are left-handed) of the cutting board, and place a kitchen towel folded into a small square in front of the bowl.

Slide your left index finger along the middle of the fillet from the head end to the tail end. You should feel the sharp ends of the pin bones sticking out from the fillet. Start from the head end and firmly hold the fillet around the first pin bone with the thumb and index finger of your left hand. Use fish tweezers to pull out the

How to
Break Down Round Fish

pin bone (20), then rinse the bone from the tweezers in the bowl of water. Tap the tweezers on the towel to dry the tips. Repeat until all the pin bones are removed.

If you started with a whole fish that weighed about 2 lb/910 g, the fillets may be about 6 in/15 cm wide at the widest part, which will be too wide to make 3-in-/7.5-cm-long slices for nigiri. You need to split the fillet in half lengthwise at the middle where the pin bones are (21). Remove the pin bones by slicing off whole units of bones (22,23) instead of pulling out each bone one by one.

Remove the skin
The skin of the fish protects the flesh from oxidation, so it is best not to remove it until just before you are ready to use the fish. Place the fillet, skin-side down, on the cutting board with the head end to the right and near the front edge of the board. Hold down the very edge of the tail end firmly with the index finger of your left hand and, still using the chef's knife, place the knife tip directly next to your fingertip (24), and slice down to the skin. When the blade reaches the skin, using a small sawing motion, gradually change the angle of the knife (25) so that the blade is flat. Now, begin cutting toward the right, between the flesh and the skin. Once there is enough skin exposed to grasp, hold the skin firmly with your left hand (26) and continue cutting until you reach the end of the fillet, separating the skin fully from the flesh.

Remove the sheet pan from the refrigerator, place this second fillet on the pan, and transfer the first fillet to the cutting board. Re-cover the sheet pan and return it to the refrigerator.

Remove the rib cage, pin bones, and skin from the first fillet
Place the fillet, skin-side down, on the cutting board, with the head end to the left and away from you and the tail end to the right and close to the front end of the cutting board. Holding the stomach side of the fillet with the four fingers of your left hand, place the tip of the knife under where the first rib-cage bone meets the pin bones, with the blade tip facing up (about the middle of the fillet). Cut and disconnect the rib-cage bone from the pin bones, then slide the knife to the next juncture of rib-cage bone and pin bones and cut and disconnect. Repeat until all the pin bones are disconnected.

Return the fillet to the sheet pan, re-cover with plastic wrap, and refrigerate until using. The head and bones can be saved for stock.

1

2

3

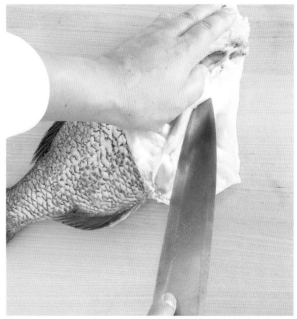

4

How to

Break Down Round Fish

5

6

9

10

11

7

8

12

13

14

How to
Break Down Round Fish

15

16

17 >>>

21

22

23

18

19

20

24

25

26

Slice Round Fish Fillet for Nigiri

These directions are for when you buy a fillet from a fish-monger, or after breaking down a whole fish. The majority of the nigiri recipes in this book require slices of fish that are about 3 in/7.5 cm long, 1 in/2.5 cm wide, and ¼ in/0.7 cm thick. But use your best judgment when it comes to how thick your cuts should be. This will depend on the type of fish, its size, and the tenderness of its flesh. For example, if the fish is chewy, cut it a bit thinner. If your fish is very tender, use our suggested thickness, or even slice it slightly thicker.

Trim the fillet

Look at the fillet you just broke down or purchased. If you started with a whole fish weighing about 1 lb/455 g and the fillets from the fish are about ½ in/12 mm thick, their width at the widest point after trimming the side edge of the fish will be about 3 in/7.5 cm. This width is perfect to make 3-in/7.5-cm slices. If you start with a purchased fillet that is more than 6 in/15 cm wide, it will be too wide to make 3-in-/7.5-cm-long slices, so you need to split the fillet in half lengthwise at the middle where the pin bones are. Remove the pin bones by slicing off whole units of bones (see photographs (22, 23) page 63) instead of pulling out each bone one by one. Remove the skin just before you start slicing the fillet for nigiri.

If the fillet is thick (for example, amberjack is usually 2 in/5 cm), place the thicker end to the right on the cutting board, skinned-side down. Using a slicing knife and keeping the blade angle parallel to the cutting board, trim off the top of the fillet horizontally from the right end to get the thickness of the bottom part of the fillet close to 1 in/2.5 cm. If the fillet is close to 2 in/5 cm, cut the thickness of the fillet in half horizontally.

Now look at the belly flap of the fillet. If the flap end is very thin, you will need to trim off the thin part to where it is at least ⅛ in/3 mm. The trimmings can be chopped and used for gunkan-maki or donburi.

Slice a thin fillet

If the fillet is less than 1 in/2.5 cm thick, follow these instructions. If it is thicker, see "Slice a 1-in/2.5-cm fillet," facing page.

Place one of the fillets on the cutting board, skinned-side down. The basic idea is that you want to slice from the thicker end of the fillet against the sinew, which runs from the head to the tail. Place the thicker side to the left on the cutting board, hold the left end with your left-hand index and middle fingers, and make slices from the left end. But consider the following before you start slicing:

You need to imagine what each fillet will yield. Visualize the knife angle you need to slice the suggested piece of fish for nigiri. You may place your slicing knife above the fillet and move it around to get the idea of the best angle to get a slice closest to 3 in/7.5 cm long. Once you get the angle right, then look at the fillet from the front to see the second angle of the knife to make about 1-in-/2.5-cm-wide slices. Once you have both angles in your mind, position the fillet appropriately on the cutting board so you can make the slice comfortably.

When making the initial cut, consider whether the end of the fish is flat or uneven. If it is uneven, the initial cut should be as thick as necessary to make a flat, even side to slice from. Make the initial cut using the slicing knife (27), using the full length of the blade from the heel to the tip in one motion (28). As you go, continually adjust the two angles of the knife to achieve the same-size slices (29,30). The tail end usually has more sinew, so if it's too chewy, chop it for gunkan-maki or donburi.

Slice a 1-in/2.5-cm fillet

If the fillet is trimmed to about 1 in/2.5 cm thick or a little thicker, place the fillet on the cutting board with the thicker end to the right. You will make slices from the right end. Again, you can move your slicing knife above the fillet to determine the angle you need in order to cut 3-in-/ 7.5-cm-long slices, but this time you don't need to adjust the second angle because your fillet is already about 1 in/2.5 cm thick.

Hold the fillet with your left-hand index and middle fingers as you make an initial cut straight down using a slicing knife, using the full length of the blade from the heel to the tip in one motion. When making the initial cut, consider whether the end of the fish is flat or a bit uneven. If it is uneven, the initial cut can be as thick as necessary to make a flat, even side to slice from. As you go, with each slice you make you will need to adjust the angle of the knife to achieve the same 3-in-/7.5-cm-long slices. When you reach the thinner part of the fillet, you will need to adjust the angle to achieve 1-in-/2.5-cm-wide slices. This time you need to turn the fillet so that the thicker side is to the left and the thin side is to the right. Continue to make slices from the left end (31,32).

How to
Slice Round Fish Fillet for Nigiri

27

28

>>>

31

32

29

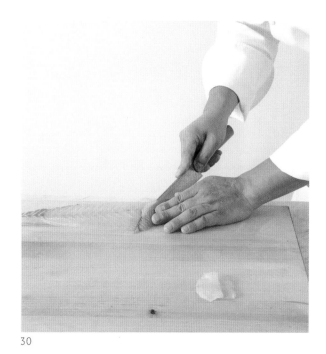

30

Slice Tender Round Fish Such as Ocean Trout and Salmon for Nigiri

Usually the basic technique is to slice the fillet against the sinew, but tender fish such as ocean trout or salmon can be sliced in the same direction as the sinew runs. This technique yields more and your slices will be more uniform. For this group of fish, cut the blocks of fish in a different direction than for round fish. The cuts are made from the back to the belly instead of from the head to the tail.

Trim the fillet

Remove the fins and trim the end of the belly flap straight. Remove the skin just before you start slicing the fillet for nigiri.

After the skin is removed, place the fillet with the skinned-side up on the cutting board to trim the blood line. The blood line runs down the center of the fillet from head to tail and is a grayish color on the surface, turning to a red-orange color inside. To remove it, make a shallow V slice from the outside edge of one side of the gray area toward the center of the fish. Repeat this slice on the other side of the gray area. If the two cuts have connected, you should be able to pull the entire piece up and discard. Remember to remove as little meat as possible.

Cut the fillet across at the edge of the head end to trim a straight line, and then make another cut 3 in/7.5 cm from the first one, basically cutting blocks of fish across the length of the body. Keep cutting the fillet in 3-in/7.5-cm intervals until the point closer to the tail where the fillet thins out too much to make a 3-in/7.5-cm piece (of even thickness). This should be about 4 in/10 cm from the end of the tail.

Slice the fillet

Place the belly side of the fillet to the right, close to the front edge of the cutting board. Look at the fillet from the front to get a visual idea of what the knife angle should be to achieve 1-in-/2.5-cm-wide slices. Using a slicing knife, slice from the left end and make the initial cut. Use the full length of the blade from the heel to the tip in one motion. As you slice, you may need to make an adjustment to the angle of the knife to achieve same-size slices. The tail end usually has more sinew; because of this you want to slice the fillet against the sinew just like other round fish. If it is too chewy, chop it for gunkan-maki or donburi.

How to
Break Down Small Fish

Atlantic mackerel (*saba*), blue mackerel (*saba*), flying fish (*tobiuo*), herring (*nishin*), horse mackerel (*aji*). Larger fish that work: arctic char (*hokkyoku iwana*), salmon (*sake*), ocean trout (*umi-masu*).

The size of the fish makes a difference in how you remove the bones and skin. Much of the process is the same, but smaller fish are more fragile, which means they must be handled a bit differently. This technique also works with larger fish that have smaller backbones, such as arctic char, salmon, and ocean trout (see How to Break Down Round Fish, page 54). Some of these fish can weigh as much as 15 lb/6.8 kg, but this technique still works because they have a thin backbone. Because these small fish are oilier and richer, their bones should not be used for stock.

Scale the fish
First, rinse the fish well under cold running water. Place the fish in a plastic bag large enough to give you room to maneuver your hands easily. The bag will help contain the flying scales, keeping any mess to a minimum. Using a fish scaler and working on one side of the fish, scrape the scales from the tail toward the head (against the direction the scales grow) to remove them. Repeat on the other side of the fish. Make sure you remove the scales near the fins. The area has many small scales, and you need to remove

> Horse mackerel has little lumps on both sides of the body close to the tail. They are a part of the scales, and very hard. Instead of using a scaler, use a chef's knife to slice from the tail toward the head. Use the scaler to remove scales on the rest of the body.

them all before you make a cut. Rinse the fish under cold running water, then check to make sure no scales remain by running your hands along the fish from the tail to the head. If you have a sink large enough for the fish to lie flat, you can dispense with the bag and scale the fish in the sink. Allow a small stream of cool tap water to run over the fish as you work, to keep the scales in the sink.

Cut off the head and remove the entrails
Place the fish on the cutting board with the head to the left and the belly facing you. (If you are left-handed, reverse the direction of the head of the fish here and equivalent directions elsewhere, and use your left hand to wield the knife throughout the instructions.) There are three points on the fish that form a line to guide you in cutting off the head. To locate the first one, run your finger along the top side of the

head toward the dorsal fin. Where you feel a change from hard bone to firm flesh, you have reached the first point. A second point is just to the right side of the pectoral fin, and the last point is just to the right side of the pelvic fin. Grab the head firmly with your left hand (if it is slippery or sharp, grip it with a kitchen towel) and place a chef's knife at a 45-degree angle toward the head of the fish. Starting the cut at the right side of the head, slice along the right side of the gill cover and pectoral fin and end just right of the pelvic fin, slicing down to the backbone. When the knife hits the backbone, change the angle of the knife to straight down and cut though the backbone but not through the fish. Turn the fish over so that the head is to the left and the dorsal fin is facing you. Using the knife at the same 45-degree angle to start, repeat the procedure in reverse, this time cutting off the head. Work carefully to avoid

How to
Break Down Small Fish

damaging the entrails. Some entrails have a strong odor and/or are extremely bitter and can contaminate the flesh.

Turn the fish over so the belly is facing you. Starting at the anus, insert the tip of the knife into the fish and draw the knife up to the head end, cutting open the belly. Remove and discard the entrails. Scrub the blood line with a small brush, like a toothbrush, and rinse the cavity with cold running water.

Fillet the fish
Clean and dry the cutting board well. Pat the fish dry with paper towels. Line a sheet pan with parchment paper. Place the fish back on the cutting board with the tail to the left, the head end to the right, and the belly facing you. Look at the head end to identify where the backbone and spines are. Place the four fingers of your left hand on the body close to the head end and apply gentle

pressure to keep the fish spines parallel to the cutting board. Use the thumb of your left hand to bring up the belly flap so the knife can be inserted under the flap without cutting it.

Starting at the head end, and keeping the knife blade parallel to the spines and the blade tip facing the tail end, use slightly downward force to make the initial cut just above the backbone (1). With a gentle sawing motion and working as closely as possible to the backbone, slide your knife toward the tail end (if the fish is large, move your hand down the fish as you move the knife), exiting at the tail end (2). As you work, you will feel the vibration on the knife if the knife is touching the backbone. Place the fillet on the prepared sheet pan (3), cover with plastic wrap, and refrigerate.

To remove the remaining fillet, place the four fingers of your left

hand on the backbone close to the head end to keep the fish spines parallel to the cutting board (4). Starting at the head end, and keeping the knife blade parallel to the spines and the blade tip facing the tail end, use slightly upward force to make the initial cut just below the backbone. With a gentle sawing motion and working as closely as possible to the backbone, slide your knife toward the tail end (5) (if the fish is large, move your hand down the fish as you move the knife), exiting at the tail end. As before, you will feel the vibration on the knife if it is touching the backbone.

Remove the rib cage
Place the fillet on the cutting board with the skin-side down, the head end to the left and slightly away from you, and the tail to the right and close to the front of the cutting board. Hold the upper left side of the

fillet stable with the four fingers of your left hand. Place the tip of the knife, with the tip facing up, under where the first rib-cage bone meets the pin bones (about the middle of the fillet). Cut and disconnect the rib-cage bone from the pin bones, then slide the knife to the next juncture of rib-cage bone and pin bones and cut and disconnect. Repeat until all the pin bones are disconnected (6).

Turn the fillet so the head side is to the right and close to the front edge of the cutting board and the belly is facing you. Hold the rib cage with the four fingers of your left hand and place the knife under the rib cage at the point where you just disconnected the pin bones. Keep the knife against the rib cage and slice it off (7).

Remove the pin bones
Place the fillet on the cutting board with the skin side down and the tail end to the left. Put a small bowl of water on the right end (or left end if you are left-handed) of the cutting board, and place a kitchen towel folded into a small square in front of the bowl.

Slide your left index finger along the middle of the fillet from the head side to the tail end. You should feel the sharp ends of the pin bones sticking out from the fillet. Start from the head end and hold the fillet around the first pin bone with the thumb and index finger of your left hand. Use fish tweezers to pull out the pin bone (8), then rinse the bone from the tweezers in the bowl of water. Tap the tweezers on the towel to dry the tips. Repeat until all the pin bones are removed.

Remove the skin
The skin of the fish protects the flesh from oxidation, so it is best not to remove it until just before you are ready to use the fish. This is especially true for fish with richer oils, such as mackerel and herring. To remove the skin from the fillet of a small fish, place the fillet on the cutting board, with the skin-side up and the tail to the right. Hold the fillet at the head end with your left hand. Using the thumbnail of your right hand and starting at the head end, begin to peel off the silver skin (9). Once you have removed about ½ in/12 mm of the skin, grasp the skin with the thumb and index finger of your right hand and continue to peel until you have removed about 1 in/2.5 cm of the skin. Now, move the index finger of your left hand forward so that it is next to the skin, peel off another 1 in/2.5 cm, and then move your left finger forward again. Continue this process until you reach the end of the fillet and the skin is completely removed. The reason you move your index finger forward as you peel away the skin is to support the fillet. If instead you try to pull off the skin all at once, the fillet may break apart.

Break Down Small Fish

You can remove the skin from the fillet of a larger fish, such as arctic char, salmon, or ocean trout, using this same method or by following the directions for removing the skin from the fillet of a round fish (see page 58). Neither method is better, but one method may be easier for you than the other. Try them both to see which one you prefer. Remove the sheet pan from the refrigerator, place this second fillet on the pan, and transfer the first fillet to the cutting board. Re-cover the sheet pan and return it to the refrigerator.

Remove the rib cage, pin bones, and skin from the first fillet

Place the fillet, skin-side down, on the cutting board, with the head end to the left and away from you and the tail end to the right and close to the front end of the cutting board. Holding the stomach side of the fillet with the four fingers of your left hand, place the tip of the knife under where the first rib-cage bone meets the pin bones, with the blade tip facing up (about the middle of the fillet). Cut and disconnect the rib-cage bone from the pin bones, then slide the knife to the next juncture of rib-cage bone and pin bones and cut and disconnect. Repeat until all the pin bones are disconnected.

Repeat the steps to remove the pin bones and skin from the first fillet, then return the fillet to the sheet pan, re-cover with plastic wrap, and refrigerate until using.

Slice Small Fish Fillet for Nigiri

These directions are for when you buy a fillet from a fish-monger, or after breaking down a whole fish. The majority of the nigiri recipes in this book require slices of fish that are about 3 in/7.5 cm long, 1 in/2.5 cm wide, and ¼ in/6 mm thick. But use your best judgment when it comes to how thick your cuts should be. This will depend on the type of fish, its size, and the tenderness of its flesh. For example, if the fish is chewy, cut it a bit thinner. If your fish is very tender, use our suggested thickness, or even slice it slightly thicker.

Look at the belly flaps of the fillets. If the flap end is very thin, you will need to trim off the thin part to a minimum ⅟₁₆-in-/2-mm-thick area. The trimming can be chopped and used for gunkan-maki or donburi. Remove the skin just before you start slicing the fillet for nigiri (see page 71).

Slice the fillet

Place one of the fillets on the cutting board, skinned-side down. The basic idea is that you want to slice from the thicker end (head end) of the fillet against the sinew, which runs from the head to the tail. Place the thicker side to the left on the cutting board, hold the left end with your left-hand index and middle fingers, and make slices from the left end. But consider the following before you start slicing:

You need to think of the yield from each fillet. The positioning of each fillet on the cutting board will depend on which fillet you are slicing. Visualize the knife angle you need to slice the suggested piece of fish for nigiri. You may place your slicing knife above the fillet and move it around to get the idea of the best angle to get a slice closest to 3 in/7.5 cm long. Once you get the angle right, look at the fillet from the side to see the second angle of the knife to make about 1-in-/2.5-cm-wide slices. Once you have both angles in your mind, you need to move the fillet to get the proper position on the cutting board for you to make the slice comfortably.

When making the initial cut, consider whether the head end of the fish is flat or a bit uneven. If it is uneven, the initial cut can be as thick as necessary to make a flat, even side to slice from. Make the initial cut using the slicing knife, using the full length of the blade from the heel to the tip in one motion. With each slice you make, you need to adjust the two angles of the knife to achieve same-size slices. The tail end usually has more sinew; if it's too chewy, chop it for gunkan-maki or donburi.

How to
Break Down Bonito (Katsuo)

bonito (*katsuo*), small tuna (*maguro*), albacore tuna (*binchomaguro/tombo*)

These directions are written for three specific fish—bonito, small tuna, and albacore tuna—that weigh 4 to 6 lb/1.8 to 2.7 kg. A delicious part of these fish that is usually thrown away in the United States is the flesh along the backbone and ribs. Once the backbone and rib cage are removed, put them on the cutting board and use a spoon to scrape off the flesh from the bones. The Japanese call this flesh *nakaochi*, or "thing from the middle." Many sushi connoisseurs prefer nakaochi to almost any other flesh from the fish. It can be used in a roll or a sushi bowl.

Find the scales and scale the fish

The scales on these fish are not like regular fish scales. They are more like shiny, hard skin. You will find the scales in three locations: first, at the top of the fish between the dorsal fin and the head; second, on the side of the fish between the middle of the body and the pectoral fin on both sides; and third, on the bottom of the belly, next to the pelvic fins.

Start by rinsing the fish well under cold running water. The fish is fragile, so be gentle as you rinse, and try not to bend it. Place the fish on a cutting board as close to the sink as possible, positioning it on its belly, with the tail toward you and the dorsal fin at the top, in a swimming position. Use a kitchen towel to grasp the tail firmly with your non-dominant hand. Place a chef's knife with the blade facing away from you at the point at which the scales start, then slice off the scales and cut off the dorsal fin. Turn the fish on its side so that the tail is still toward you and its belly is to the right. Starting just in front of the pectoral fin, slice the scales off. Turn the fish again so that the belly is up, and slice off the scales near the pelvic fin. Turn the fish to the last side, belly to the left, and remove the scales around the pectoral fin.

Cut off the head

Place the fish on the cutting board with the head to the left and the belly toward you. (If you are left-handed, reverse the direction of the head of the fish here and equivalent directions elsewhere, and use your left hand to wield the knife throughout the instructions.) Imagine a line that runs from the top of the head through the right side of the pectoral fin and then ends at the right side of the pelvic fin. Hold the head of the fish with a kitchen towel and, using the chef's knife, follow that line, cutting across the back of the head to the backbone at a 45-degree angle to the left. When you reach the backbone, change the angle of the knife so the blade is straight down and cut through the backbone. Turn the fish over so the dorsal side is toward you. Make the same cut, but start at the pelvic fin and cut to the head. Work carefully to avoid damaging the entrails. Some entrails have a strong odor and/or are extremely bitter and can contaminate the flesh.

Remove the entrails

Turn the fish over so the belly is facing you. Starting at the anus,

Whether you are breaking down a bonito or a tuna, reserve the head, which is delicious roasted. It is difficult to cut it in half, so you may have to take it to your butcher and ask if he or she will split it with a band saw. Roast it in a 350°F/180°C oven until the flesh is tender; the timing will depend on the size of the head. When it is ready, you will be able to pick most of the meat from the head easily. Enjoy it with ponzu sauce (see page 119) and spicy grated daikon (see page 121).

Break Down Bonito (Katsuo)

How to

insert the tip of the knife into the fish and draw the knife up to the head end, cutting open the belly. When you removed the head from the body, some of the entrails most likely came away with the head. Open the belly flap and remove any entrails that remain. In the cavity, behind where the entrails sat, you will see a dark red line where the backbone and rib cage meet. This is the blood line and must be removed. Use a small spoon to scrape out as much of the blood line as possible. Then, rinse the outside and the cavity of the fish under cold running water and scrub the cavity gently with a small brush, like a toothbrush.

Portion the loin

Clean and dry the cutting board well. Pat the fish dry with paper towels. Line a sheet pan with parchment paper. Place the fish on the cutting board, with the tail

to the left, the belly facing you, and the head end away from you at a 45-degree angle. Hold the top of the body with your left hand and place the knife at the anus, with the knife pointing toward the tail. The knife should cut just above the anal fin and the finlets. Inside the fins are very small bones that radiate out from the spine to the top and bottom of the fish. On the outside they look like small arrowheads in a line from behind the anal fin. Cut toward the backbone, feeling the spine just under the blade as you work. You can do this in one or two passes, until you feel the knife along the backbone.

Turn the fish counterclockwise so that the head is to the lower left, the back is facing you, and the tail is away from you at a 45-degree angle. Hold the knife facing left at the tail end of the body, just above the finlets, and keep the blade almost parallel to

the cutting board. Cut toward the head end, feeling the neural spines just under the blade. The blade should be just above the finlets and dorsal fin muscles. Make the cut all the way to the head end. Now, make one more pass with the knife, carefully holding the loin up just enough with your thumb so that you can get the tip of the blade to the backbone, and cut the backbone free. The final cut is to remove the fish from the tail: hold the fish up at the tail end so that you can insert the blade facing the tail, then make the cut to release the loin from the tail. Gently transfer the loin, skin-side up, to the prepared sheet pan, cover with plastic wrap, and refrigerate. It is important to lay the loin skin-side up because it is rounded. If you place it skin-side down, the loin will flatten out under its own weight. This will cause the meat of the fish to break from its own weight.

Remove the backbone

Keep the fish in the same position, with its head to the lower left, the back facing you, and the tail away from you at a 45-degree angle. Place the tip of the knife blade at the tail end of the body just underneath the finlets. Keeping the angle of the blade almost parallel to the cutting board, start to cut toward the head, feeling the spine just above the blade. The blade should be just under all the finlets and dorsal fin muscles and should run along the backbone to the head end.

Turn the fish counterclockwise so that tail is to the left and the head end is away from you at a 45-degree angle. Place the blade just under the anal fin and cut open the skin toward the tail. The blade should run just underneath all of the finlets and then all of the way to the backbone. Now that the backbone is free at the tail end, gently lift the end of the bone with

your left hand, place your knife blade under the backbone facing the head side, and cut and disconnect the rib cage from the backbone. Remove the backbone.

Trim the loin

Place the loin on the cutting board so that the head end is facing you, skin-side down, and the tail is away from you. Remove the rib cage by slicing at an angle just underneath the bones from the center of the loin to the left. To find the small bones, run the index finger of your left hand from the tail to the head end along the center of the fish where the dark flesh is located (where the backbone was). Place the tip of the knife at the center of the tail end and slice straight down along the line where the backbone was, ending at the head end and splitting the loin in two. Keep the group of small bones on only one of the loins. To remove the group of small bones, run the

knife against the loin between the small bones and the flesh, from the tail end to the head end. Last, cut off the thin belly flap.

Remove the sheet pan from the refrigerator and transfer the reserved loin to the cutting board. Place the two small loins onto the pan, re-cover, and refrigerate. Trim the large loin into two small loins and refrigerate, covered, until needed.

To skin the loin, follow the directions for skinning round fish fillets on page 58, removing the skin just before you are ready to use the fish.

If you will be using the bonito loins for tataki (see How to Make Seared Bonito, page 78), leave the skin intact.

How to
Make Seared Bonito (Katsuo no Tataki)

Tataki, a traditional Japanese technique for preparing bonito, was adopted by chefs in the United States many years ago. It calls for briefly searing a loin, then slicing it and seasoning with ginger, garlic, herbs, and ponzu. But it lends itself to more than just bonito. Tuna and albacore are also commonly prepared this way and then usually added to a salad or served on their own as sashimi with some soy sauce and wasabi. You can use this technique on beef, as well, preferably a cut like flank steak or New York strip steak, which is delicious served as carpaccio or over roasted vegetables.

Prepare the bonito loin for tataki

If you started with a whole fish weighing 4 to 6 lb/1.8 to 2.7 kg as suggested, then the loins from the fish will be triangular, about 2½ in/6 cm tall at the thickest part. If the loin is larger, refer to How to Slice Tuna for Nigiri (page 81) to cut brick-shaped pieces from the loin.

There are three ways to sear the bonito loin: with a kitchen torch, in a cast-iron pan (that can fit the loin without bending it) on the stove top, or on a grill. It is important that after the loin has been seared, you either immediately place it in the refrigerator to cool (this way retains more of the smoky flavor) or plunge it into a bowl of ice water, then remove and pat dry. Cover with plastic wrap and refrigerate until using.

The kitchen-torch method

The torch is the easiest method because it gives you the most control. Place a metal rack on a sheet pan, and put the bonito loin, skin-side up, on the rack. Using a sweeping motion and holding the torch about 3 in/7.5 cm above the loin, sear the skin side first until dark brown, then sear all sides, but not the ends, of the loin evenly to a medium brown, leaving the interior raw. (The interior is visible from the ends. There will be two, three, or four sides, depending on the size of the whole fish before it was broken down.) With this method, you get the smokiness and almost the same texture as with the traditional method (on the grill), but you don't have to move the fragile loin as much.

The stove-top method

For the second method, you will need a bonito loin with the skin intact that is just smaller than your cast-iron skillet, so you have enough space in the pan to maneuver the loin. Preheat the cast-iron pan over high heat. When it is hot, add a small amount of vegetable oil and tilt the pan to spread the oil evenly over the bottom of the pan. Add the loin, skin-side down, and sear until dark brown. Then sear all sides, but not the ends, of the loin evenly to a medium brown, leaving the interior raw. (The interior is visible from the ends.)

The grill method

Finally, the traditional way to sear the bonito loin calls for a grill and is how people in Japan have been making tataki for centuries. It gives the fish a smoky flavor, and the contrast of the cooked exterior and the raw interior gives the preparation a unique texture and flavor.

Make a fire in a hibachi or other grill with dry rice straw. Place the loin, skin-side down, on the cutting board. Insert five

12-in-/30-cm-long metal skewers into the loin equidistant from one another to distribute the weight of the loin. Position the skewers so they radiate out in a fan shape at different angles so that you can grasp them and maneuver the loin over the fire.

Firmly holding the skewers with a towel, place the loin, skin-side down, over the fire and cook until dark brown. The timing will depend on the intensity of the fire, but it should take about 20 seconds. Carefully flip the loin over and cook the other side until the surface of the flesh turns opaque, about 10 seconds, leaving the interior raw. (The interior is visible from the ends.)

How to
Slice Bonito (Katsuo), Seared Bonito (Katsuo no Tataki), or Small Tuna (Maguro) for Nigiri

These directions are for after breaking down a whole fish weighing 4 to 6 lb/1.8 to 2.7 kg as suggested or purchasing a small loin from your fishmonger. The loins from this size fish are between 2 to 2½ in/5 to 6 cm at the tallest part. If the loin is larger, refer to How to Slice Tuna for Nigiri (facing page). Because these loins are so small, it is not necessary to cut them into the brick-shaped pieces of larger tuna or albacore we usually slice from. The resulting slices will be triangular. This is a common way of cutting fish for sushi or sashimi from the smaller loins of these fish. The majority of the nigiri recipes in this book require fish slices of this type that are about 3 in/7.5 cm long, 1 in/2.5 cm wide, and ⅜ in/1 cm thick. Use your best judgment when it comes to how thick your cuts should be. This will depend on the type of fish, its size, and the tenderness of its flesh. If the fish is chewy, cut it a bit thinner. If your fish is very tender, use our suggested thickness, or even slice it slightly thicker.

Slice the loin for nigiri

Place the skinned loin on the cutting board, skinned-side down (if tataki, place the loin skin-side up) with the head end to the left. Place your slicing knife above the left end of the loin and move the knife around to get the idea of the best angle to get a slice closest to 3 in/ 7.5 cm long. Once you have the angle in your mind, you need to move the loin to get the proper position on the cutting board for you to make the slice comfortably. Hold the head end of the loin with your left-hand index and middle fingers, and make the slices from the left end.

When making the initial cut, consider whether the end of the fish is flat or a bit uneven. If it is uneven, the initial cut can be as thick as necessary to make a flat, even side to slice from. Make the initial cut using the slicing knife, using the full length of the blade from the heel to the tip in one motion. As you go, adjust the angle of the knife blade to achieve 3-in-/7.5-cm-long and ⅜-in-/1-cm-thick slices. The tail end usually has more sinew; if it's too chewy, chop it for gunkan-maki or donburi.

How to

Slice Tuna (Maguro) for Nigiri

These are the directions for portioning a large chunk of tuna or albacore loin into the brick-shaped pieces from which slices are taken to make nigiri. The photographs of the process on pages 85–91 show a tuna that is much larger than needed, but it is easier to see the technique. If you would like to purchase a smaller chunk of tuna to break down in the same way, it would need to be approximately 1½ in/4 cm thick and the sides should be approximately 6 in/15 cm. This is large enough so that the tuna piece can stand like you see in the photos. It will give you more than you need for a few orders of sushi. Another option is to purchase a tuna steak, approximately 8 oz/225 g, which is a triangular shape with about 5½-in-/14-cm-long sides and about 1 in/2.5 cm thick. The technique for cutting this piece of tuna is different; you will keep the tuna steak flat on the cutting board to process. It is the easiest way, and you don't end up buying much more than you need. In most cases, tuna at a fish market is sold skinless, but we have shown how to remove the skin, just in case.

When purchasing tuna, be sure to ask if it is sushi-grade and when they got it in. Be sure to look at the fish; does it look moist? It should look fresh and a bit moist, but not wet or pale. It shouldn't be in water or directly sitting on ice. It should look like fresh red meat. It is difficult to suggest a size or weight to purchase for nigiri; no matter what, you will have more than you need. Look for a piece that is from the center of the loin and closer to the head side of the tuna so that it will have less sinew. If you are using a tuna loin from a whole small tuna, refer to How to Slice Bonito, Seared Bonito, or Small Tuna for Nigiri (facing page) on how to cut it for nigiri.

How to
Slice Tuna (Maguro) for Nigiri

Portion the tuna loin into brick-shaped pieces to slice for nigiri

At a Japanese grocery store, you may be able to purchase brick-shaped sushi-grade tuna already cleaned and portioned to slice for nigiri. If you start with this brick-shaped piece, begin at "Slice the brick-shaped pieces for nigiri" (facing page).

Line a sheet pan with parchment paper. Place the tuna loin on the cutting board with the cut end facing you and the skin to the left. Using a chef's knife, place the knife between the skin and flesh at the top of the loin (1), keep the tip of the knife against the skin, and slice and peel off the skin (2).

Place the tuna loin on the cutting board, skinned-side down.

Look at the loin from the cut end. It is almost a triangle. One of the bottom corners will have more sinew (which corner depends on which fillet it is). Place the loin on the cutting board with the cut side facing you and the sinewy corner to the right.

Place the blade of the knife along the top of the sinewy corner where the thickest sinew is (3). The sinew is visible as very pronounced white lines going through the meat of the tuna. Make a slice from there toward the cutting board at about a 45-degree angle to the left (4), following the top of the sinew. Your knife will reach the cutting board near the middle of the bottom of the loin (5).

Remove the sinewy fillet to the parchment-lined sheet pan. In most cases, the sinewy piece of tuna is very difficult to clean pieces out to make sushi from. A better option is to use a spoon and scrape the meat from the sinew (1ST–4ST). It comes off fairly easily and is delicious, so

it shouldn't be wasted. It can then be chopped and used for gunkan-maki or donburi.

Using a slicing knife, remove the blood line, which looks like a dark red half-oval on one side of the tuna loin. Its size changes depending on how far down the tuna loin you are working. Carefully, so as not to remove any of the tuna flesh, remove the blood line. Place the knife blade along the top of the blood line (6) and with a slicing motion follow the line of blood in an arcing cut, ending with the knife coming out at the lower end of the blood line. Discard the blood line.

If there is a significant difference in the size between one end of the loin and the other end (7), we suggest cutting the loin to create more uniform sizes (8, 9). Where you cut will depend on the shape of the loin. The idea is to get uniform-size pieces without a lot of waste.

Look at the loin from the cut side (10). You need to figure out how many 3-by-1¼-in/7.5-by-3-cm rectangles you can get; it's almost like a puzzle. Having a piece of paper cut to 3 by 1¼ in/ 7.5 by 3 cm may help you to visualize the size you are trying to cut and give you an idea of the yield (11–13). The piece of the loin in the photos shows one side of the loin is almost 6 in/15 cm from bottom to tip, so we slice off a 1¼-in-/3-cm-thick piece from the side (14). Then, we cut the piece in half (15) to make two slice-ready pieces (16). From the thicker side of the remaining loin (which is now about 3 in/7.5 cm tall), cut a 1¼-in-/3-cm-thick slice from the side, cutting almost straight down (17,18), then keep repeating the same 1¼-in-/3-cm-thick slice (19–21). The very last remaining piece of tuna may be too small to get slices for nigiri from. If so, chop it and use it for gunkan-maki or donburi.

Slice the brick-shaped pieces for nigiri

The tuna slices for nigiri in this book should be about 3 by 1¼ by ⅜ in/7.5 by 3 by 1 cm, but this is just one of the basic measurement options. Depending on the size of your tuna, and which section of the tuna you get, you need to adjust the dimensions. For example, if the tuna is a little chewy, cut the slices a little thinner. If the tuna is very tender, you can keep the same thickness we suggested or even slice a little thicker.

If the brick-shaped piece of the tuna you just portioned is 3 by 1¼ by 6 in/7.5 by 3 by 15 cm, place the 6-in/15-cm side of the loin horizontally on the cutting board (22). Slice from the right end, holding the fillet from the top near the end with your left-hand index and middle fingers (23). Using a slicing knife, and with the full length of the blade from the

heel to the tip in one motion (24), slice straight down in the suggested thickness (25–27).

If the piece of tuna is thinner than 1¼ in/3 cm or narrower than 3 in/7.5 cm, look at the piece and visualize the knife angle you need to slice the suggested size piece for nigiri. You may place your slicing knife above the piece of tuna and move it around to get the idea of the best angle to get a slice closest to 3 in/7.5 cm long. Once you get the angle right, look at the piece from the front to see the second angle of the knife to make about 1¼-in-/3-cm-wide slices. Once you have both angles in your mind, you need to move the fish to get the proper position on the cutting board for you to make the slice comfortably. Hold the left end with your left-hand index and middle fingers, and make slices from the left end. When making the initial cut, consider whether the end of the fish is flat

How to
Slice Tuna (Maguro) for Nigiri

or a bit uneven. If it is uneven, the initial cut can be as thick as necessary to make a flat even side to slice from. Make the initial cut, using the full length of the blade from the heel to the tip in one motion. As you go, adjust the angle of the knife blade to achieve same-size slices.

Slicing a tuna steak for nigiri

If possible, ask your fishmonger to cut a new steak from the center of the loin closer to the head end, which has less sinew than the tail end. The steak should be approximately 8 oz/225 g, triangular in shape, with sides about 5½ in/14 cm wide and 1 in/2.5 cm thick, without the skin.

Place the steak flat on the cutting board. If there is strong sinew and/or a blood line, use a slicing knife to trim it off. In most cases, a sinewy piece of tuna is very difficult to clean pieces out of for sushi. A better option is to use a

spoon and scrape the meat from the sinew (1ST–4ST). It comes off fairly easily and is delicious, so it shouldn't be wasted. It can then be chopped and used for gunkan-maki or donburi.

Place the blood line side close to the front end of the cutting board and the sinew side away from you. Slice from the left, placing the knife above the steak and moving it around to get the idea of the best angle to get a slice closest to 3 in/7.5 cm long. Once you get the angle right, look at the steak from the front to see the second angle of the knife to make about 1¼-in-/3-cm-wide slices. Once you have both angles in your mind, position the steak on the cutting board so you can make the slice comfortably. Hold the left end with your left-hand index and middle fingers, and make slices from the left end.

When making the initial cut, consider whether the end of the fish is flat or a bit uneven. If it is uneven, the initial cut can be as thick as necessary to make a flat even side to slice from. Make the initial cut, using the full length of the blade from the heel to the tip in one motion. As you go, adjust the two angles of the knife blade to achieve same-size slices.

1

2

3

4

How to
Slice Tuna (Maguro) for Nigiri

5

6

>>>

9

10

7

8

11

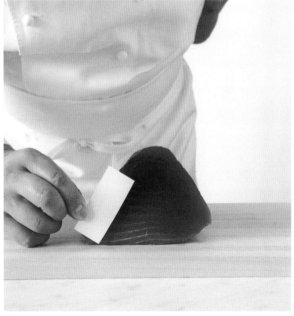

12

How to
Slice Tuna (Maguro) for Nigiri

13

14 >>>

17

18

15

16

19

20

Slice Tuna (Maguro) for Nigiri

21

22

>>>

25

26

23

24

27

How to

Scrape Tuna (Maguro)

1ST

2ST

3ST

4ST

How to

Break Down Sardines (Iwashi)

Sardines are both easy and difficult to prepare for sushi. They are small, and if you use the technique described here, the tiny bones will come out easily with the backbone. But sardines are also a very soft fish and break easily. It is important to work carefully and in small steps. This is not a process you can rush through. It is worth every minute, however, and it is much easier to remove the bones with this technique than with a knife.

It is important to keep sardines on ice as you are working with them. Fill a shallow bowl with ice, cover with plastic wrap, and whenever you are not working on a sardine or on a part of a sardine, lay it on the plastic wrap over the ice. It is also important to prepare the sardines as close to the time you will serve them as possible. Sardines start to oxidize the minute you begin to work with them, and the fat from the fish can heighten the fishy smell rather quickly.

Scale the fish
Rinse the sardine under cold running water. Place a small cutting board in the sink where the water from the faucet will hit it directly, and turn on the water so that it flows in a very small stream. Place the sardine, with the head to the left, on the board so that the water is hitting it, and hold the fish with your left hand. (If you are left-handed, reverse the direction of the head of the

fish here and equivalent directions elsewhere, and use your left hand to wield the knife and perform other dominant actions throughout the instructions.) With the back of a small utility knife held at a 90-degree angle, gently slide the knife from the tail toward the head (against the direction the scales grow) to remove the scales. Repeat on the other side of the fish. Be gentle, as sardines are quite fragile. The water should keep the scales from flying out of the sink.

Cut off the head and remove the entrails
Rinse and dry the cutting board. Place the sardine on the board with the head still pointing left and the belly facing you. Imagine a line that runs from the top of the head to the right side of the gill cover and pelvic fins. Cut along this line, and then cut off and discard the head. Turn the sardine

so that the head end is facing you, the tail is away from you, and the stomach is to the right. Starting at the anus, make a cut straight down along the belly of the fish, cutting on the left side of the pelvic fin all the way to the head end. This will cut off the bottom of the fish belly and expose the entrails. Use the tip of the knife to scrape out the entrails, then rinse the cavity with cold running water.

Fillet the fish
Clean and dry the cutting board well. Pat the fish dry with a paper towel. Fill a shallow bowl or a platter with ice and cover with plastic wrap. Check the sardine for any scales that were missed and remove any you find. Place the sardine on the cutting board close to the front edge, with the tail to the left, the head end away from you at a 45-degree angle, and the dorsal fin facing you. Hold the sardine down with your left-hand index and middle fingers.

How to
Break Down Sardines (Iwashi)

Along the back side of the sardine, make a shallow incision (1), starting at the head end, going over the top of the dorsal fin, and finishing just past the dorsal fin. Do not cut completely into the flesh of the fish. Repeat this cut, but go under the dorsal fin this time (2).

Place the tip of the index finger of your right hand, nail-side up and pad-side down, into the incision at the head end, making sure your finger is touching the backbone (3). Feeling the backbone and neural spines under your fingertip, slide your finger to the left all the way to the tail. Next, return to the head end and insert the same finger in the same spot, but this time your fingertip should pass the middle bone by about ½ in/12 mm. Slide your finger all the way to the tail again (4), keeping it very close to the middle bone, so that your finger is almost scraping it and you can lift the fillet (5). You should now have one whole fillet separated

from the fish (6). If the fillet is still connected in a few spots, run a small knife between the two fillets to release the first fillet. Place the fillet without the backbone on the bowl of ice.

Place the other fillet on the cutting board with the backbone-side down, the head end to the left, the tail to the right, and the dorsal fin facing you. Hold the end of the backbone with the fingers of your left hand and place the index finger of your right hand in the other incision you made before removing the first fillet. You should be able to feel the neural spines on the pad of your fingertip and the fillet on the top of your fingertip. This time slide your finger to the right all the way to the tail (7) to detach the fillet from the backbone (8). Discard the backbone. Take a good look at the two fillets to see if any small fin bones or rib-cage bones are left behind. If you detect some, carefully slice them off with your

knife (9). Try to remove as little flesh as possible. Keep the fillets on the bowl of ice, covered with plastic wrap, when not working with them.

There is a good reason to fillet a sardine this way. If you look at the backbone that has been removed, you will see many tiny neural spines rising from it. If you used a knife to separate the fillets from the backbone, you would leave all those bones in the fillet, and they are difficult to remove.

Remove the skin
Place a fillet on the cutting board, with the skin-side up and the tail to the right. Hold the fillet at the head end with your left hand. Using the thumbnail of your right hand and starting at the head end, begin to peel off the silver skin. Once you have removed about ½ in/12 mm of the skin, grasp the skin with the thumb and index finger of your right hand and continue to peel

until you have removed about 1 in/2.5 cm of the skin. Now, move the index finger of your left hand forward so that it is next to the skin, peel off another 1 in/2.5 cm, and then move your left finger forward again. Continue this process until you reach the end of the fillet and the skin is completely removed (10). The reason you move your index finger forward as you peel away the skin is to support the fillet. If instead you tried to pull off the skin all at once, the fillet might break apart. Keep the fillets on the bowl of ice, covered with plastic wrap, when not working with them.

Repeat with the second fillet, then place both fillets on the bowl of ice, cover with more plastic wrap, and refrigerate until using.

How to
Break Down Sardines (Iwashi)

1

2

>>>

5

6

3

4

7

8

How to
Break Down Sardines (Iwashi)

9

10

How to

Break Down Eel

These instructions are for both saltwater eel and freshwater eel. We prefer small saltwater eels weighing only about 6 oz/170 g, because the bones of the rib cage are small enough to eat. The size of the head should be a little smaller than your thumb. For freshwater eels, we look for ones weighing about 1½ lb/680 g.

Remove the slippery coating
Rinse the eel with cold running water. Eels do not have scales, but they do have a slippery coating that makes them difficult to handle. To remove it, place the eel in a medium-size bowl, sprinkle with about 2 tbsp kosher salt, and massage the salt into the skin of the eel to remove the coating. Rinse again under cold running water and pat dry with paper towels.

Remove the entrails
Place the eel horizontally on a cutting board, with the head to the right, the tail to the left, and the stomach facing you and about 2 in/5 cm away from the front edge of the board. (These directions are written for a right-handed person. If you are left-handed, reverse the references.) The head should be almost at the edge of the board. Secure the eel head in position by hammering a nail through its eye into the cutting board.

Use a small utility knife to cut open the stomach. Place the tip of the knife into the middle of the throat and slice open the skin by sliding the knife to the anus, located about three-fourths of the way down the belly side. Cut the esophagus directly next to the head and remove the innards. Wipe out the cavity with paper towels.

Cut off the head and fillet the eel
Line a sheet pan with parchment paper. Place the knife vertically next to the head, and make a cut right behind the head down to the backbone. Reposition the knife so that the blade faces the tail, and cut along the backbone down to the end of the eel, finishing out the tail end. Do not cut all the way through the eel. Instead, just cut along the bone, much like you would if you were butterflying a fish. Gently flip the top piece of the eel over onto the cutting board so that you can see the backbone

that is still connected to the fillet. Place the tip of the knife under the bone right next to the head, and again, using the bone for guidance, move the tip of the knife to the left to slice out the backbone. This will be easy since you can see the bone clearly, plus the natural shape of the eel lifts the bone up for easy access. You should end up with a whole eel with no backbone. Set the backbone aside.

Cut off the head, remove the nail, and reserve the head with the backbone. Turn the eel over and slice off the fins on its back. The eel is now filleted with the two fillets still attached. Place the eel on the parchment-lined pan, cover with plastic wrap, and refrigerate until using. Place the eel backbone and head in an airtight container and refrigerate for making the eel braising liquid on page 152.

How to
Break Down Squid (Ika)

Purchase squid with bodies that are about 4 in/10 cm long, not including the tentacles. These directions are for preparing squid for sushi (or sashimi), but other parts of the squid can be saved for using in other ways. For example, you can cure the innards in salt for two days, then pat them dry and pack them in a mixture of mirin and miso for about a week to make the delicious condiment known as *shiokara*.

Remove the head

Rinse the squid under cold running water. Grasp the squid tentacles in one hand and the body in the other, and with a slight twisting motion, firmly pull apart. The head and entrails should slip easily from the body. Set the body aside. Position the blade of a slicing knife or utility knife between the eyes and bottom of the tentacles and cut straight down, then discard everything above the tentacles (or reserve for another use). Once the tentacles are cut from the head, you will find the beak in the middle of the base of the tentacles. The squid beak is a bony piece of inedible cartilage, usually dark brown to black. Squeeze the sides of the base of the tentacles and the beak should easily pop out. Discard the beak and set the tentacles aside.

Clean the body

Grasp the tubelike body portion, which contains a thin, clear sliver of cartilage (sometimes called the quill) that is almost the same length as the body. Using your fingertips, pull the cartilage from the open end of the body and discard it. If you want to remove the mottled purplish skin from the body, grasp one end of the body and, using a clean kitchen towel, gently press down on the body with the towel and slide the towel to the opposite end of the body. The skin will easily separate from the body. You can leave the skin intact, if you like, though most cooks choose to remove it for a more appealing presentation. The skin on larger squid should be removed, however, because it is often tough. When you remove the skin, the little "wings" at the closed end of the squid body often come off as well. If this happens, you can use them as you use the tentacles.

Once you have removed the skin, thoroughly rinse the inside of the body tube with water, using your finger to pull out any residual entrails. Pat the tube and tentacles dry, wrap in plastic wrap, and refrigerate until using.

You can also reserve the squid ink sac, which looks like a black vein and is located among the entrails. Gently lift up the entrails and you will find the ink sac in a tube. Carefully cut the tube about ½ in/12 mm above and below the ink sac to free the sac. If you work carefully, the sac will not break. To extract the ink, hold the sac over a small bowl, puncture the sac, and then squeeze it to release the ink, which will flow out easily. Transfer the ink to a small airtight container and, if you are not using it immediately, freeze until needed. The ink can be used for a sauce or vinaigrette or it can be cooked with rice.

How to

Break Down Geoduck Clam (Mirugai)

When people see these big burrowing clams for the first time, their large siphon and big shell often prompt a double take. But despite their formidable appearance, they are fairly easy to break down and make excellent nigiri and sashimi.

In a large pot, bring 4 qt/3.8 L water to a boil. Have ready a large bowl of ice water. Meanwhile, rinse the geoduck under cold running water to remove any sand or other impurities.

Peel the clam
Place the geoduck in the boiling water and blanch for 15 seconds. Immediately transfer to the ice water to halt the cooking. Remove from the ice water and peel off the outer skin on the siphon (the part that looks like an elephant trunk) and the body.

Separate the meat from the shell
Place the clam on a cutting board, with the body to the left, the siphon to the right, and the shell flat. (If you are left-handed, reverse the direction of the body and siphon here and equivalent directions elsewhere, and use your left hand to wield the knife throughout the instructions.) Holding the shell tightly,

slide a small knife blade into the clam between the shell and body and cut the body away from the shell. Repeat on the other side, to disconnect the clam body from the shell. Cut off and remove the entrails. Cut off the siphon at its base to remove it from the body. Put the body into an airtight container and refrigerate for another use. For sushi you need only the siphon. Split the siphon in half lengthwise, then rinse under cold running water to remove any sand and impurities. Pat dry with a paper towel, wrap in plastic wrap, and refrigerate until using.

Slice the siphon
To slice the siphon for nigiri, place half of it, cut-side down, on a cutting board, with the large end to the left. Carefully hold the large end of the siphon half with the flat of your left hand lying against its outside edge. Using a slicing knife, cut the large end from top to bottom on the diagonal, feeling the

clam through your hand to ensure an even slice. The piece should be about 3 in/7.5 cm long, 1 in/2.5 cm wide, and 3/16 in/4 mm thick. With each slice you make, you need to adjust the knife to achieve same-size pieces.

Sometimes the siphon can be a little too crunchy to eat without additional cuts, so taste a small piece. If you think it is too crunchy, use a small knife to make little incisions about 1/4 in/6 mm apart along the outer edge of each slice.

How to

Break Down and Cook Octopus (Tako)

You won't find this technique in a European cookbook; they wouldn't use green tea to lend octopus an attractive color. Massaging the octopus with salt is another important part of the preparation, as is getting every little bit of residue out of the suction cups. These steps are a lot of work, but they make a world of difference in the flavor and texture of the meat. You can use this technique every time you cook octopus; even for grilling or stewing, it will result in tender, flavorful octopus.

One 2-lb/910-g fresh whole octopus

1¼ to 2 oz/35 to 55 g salt (3 to 5 percent of the weight of the octopus)

3 tbsp loose Japanese green tea

In a large stockpot over high heat, bring 3 gl/11 L water to a boil. Prepare an ice bath in a bowl large enough to submerge the entire octopus.

Meanwhile, rinse the octopus under cold running water for a few minutes to remove any liquid or particles. Place it in a large bowl, and cover with the salt. Massage the octopus very firmly for about 15 minutes to exfoliate the slippery slime on the surface and tenderize the meat. Using a toothpick, pipe cleaner, or small brush, clean the inside of each suction cup.

Turn the body inside out and pull away the entrails, the plastic-like bony sticks, and the stomach sac. Discard. Turn the octopus right-side out. Wash the octopus inside and out again with cold running water.

Place the tea in the pot of boiling water, lower the heat, and simmer for 3 minutes. Hold the body of the octopus firmly and dip the tentacles in the simmering water for 5 seconds (be careful not to burn yourself; if necessary, you can run a skewer through the body and thread a loop of kitchen twine through the holes to create a handle for the body). Bring it up out of the water, wait a few seconds, then dip the tentacles back into the simmering water again. Repeat five times. The tentacles will curl more with every dip. After six dips, submerge the entire body in the water. Turn off the heat, and let the octopus rest in the water for 5 minutes. Remove the octopus from the hot water and shock it in the large bowl of ice water until completely cooled. Pat dry, cover, and refrigerate until using.

How to
Slice Octopus (Tako) for Nigiri from Whole Octopus

If you are using a store-purchased octopus leg, start at Slice the Tentacle, below.

Remove the tentacles

Place the octopus on your cutting board, tentacle-side down with the body to the top.

Hold the head with your left hand in an upright position. (These directions are written for a right-handed person. If you are left-handed, reverse the references.) Place the slicing-knife blade tip just below the eyes. Keeping the blade parallel to the cutting board, slice the head free from the tentacles. Now slice the head free from the body just above the eyes and discard the head. Set the body aside for another use (see Note).

Flip the tentacles upside down. You will see the mouth in the center. Place the knife in between two tentacles and slice toward the mouth. Repeat with the next set of the tentacles to free one tentacle. You can remove them all in this manner, or just what you need. Discard the mouth and the area around it.

Slice the tentacle

Place one of the tentacles onto the cutting board with the thicker side to the left. Hold the left end of the tentacle with your left-hand index and middle fingers. You want to make slices that are as close as possible to 3 by 1 by $^3/_{16}$ in/7.5 by 2.5 by 0.5 cm (see How to Slice Small Fish Fillet for Nigiri, page 74). Visualize the knife angle you need to slice a piece this size. Using the full length of the blade from the heel to tip, make the slice. As you approach the thin end of the tentacle, the angle of the blade will become more horizontal to keep the thickness and the length of the slices the same. Eventually you will be unable to make slices of the needed width, but keep slicing until the end. Sometimes you need to use two skinny slices to make one nigiri. We like this best; it has the most unique look and texture.

The body is a delicious part of the octopus but does not work for sushi. Since the octopus is so lightly cooked, you can use it in many ways, such as grilled and added to a Mediterranean-style salad. It is great in a tomato-based pasta sauce, but you will need to cook it a lot longer. Octopus is tender when blanched or lightly cooked but after that it has to cook for a long time to become tender. A traditional Japanese way to serve it is in a cucumber and seaweed *sunomono* (vinegared salad); just slice thinly and add to the sunomono.

Vinegar-cured Mackerel (Shime Saba)

Most sushi bars have cured mackerel, or *shime saba*, on their menu, and each sushi chef has a different technique and recipe for making it. Some sushi chefs cure the mackerel with sugar first instead of salt. Some briefly rinse the mackerel in vinegar, and others marinate it in vinegar. Some diners prefer the flavor of the fish the same day it has been marinated, and others like how the fish tastes a day later, after the flavor has developed and matured. These are personal preferences. Because the taste of sushi prepared with shime saba is very close to how the earliest sushi tasted (see page 11), whenever you eat shime saba, you are reminded of the long history of sushi.

1 piece kelp for dashi, 3 by 2 in/7.5 by 5 cm

½ cup/120 ml rice vinegar

1 tbsp mirin

1 tbsp sugar

2 tsp light soy sauce

1 tsp peeled and julienned fresh ginger

3 lemon slices, each ⅛ in/3 mm thick

1 whole Atlantic or blue mackerel, about 1 lb/455 g or 13 in/33 cm long

4 tsp kosher salt

Have ready a bowl half filled with ice water. If you see some dust on the kelp, wipe it off lightly with a paper towel before use. In a small saucepan, combine the kelp, vinegar, mirin, sugar, soy sauce, and ginger and place over medium heat. Bring to a boil, remove from the heat, and add the lemon slices. Place the pan in the bowl of ice water until cool. Set aside.

Follow the directions in How to Break Down Small Fish (see page 69) until the mackerel is in three parts (two fillets and the backbone). Discard the backbone. Do not remove the rib cage or the skin.

Sprinkle 1 tsp of the salt evenly over each side of each fillet. Place the fillets on a nonreactive sheet pan, cover with plastic wrap, and refrigerate for 2 hours. After 2 hours, remove the fillets from the refrigerator, rinse under cold running water, and pat dry with paper towels to remove the excess moisture. Place the fish on a rimmed sheet pan just large enough to hold both fillets flat and in a single layer, and pour the cooled marinade over the fish. Cover and marinate in the refrigerator for 30 minutes.

Remove the fillets from the marinade and pat dry with paper towels. Continue with the directions in How to Break Down Small Fish, starting with removing the rib cage and pin bones. Carefully trim a little of the belly so that it is closer to being a straight line. Wrap in plastic wrap and refrigerate until using. Peel off the skin just before using. To cut the fillets for nigiri, see the directions in How to Slice Small Fish Fillet for Nigiri (page 74).

How to
Make Sushi Rice (Sushi-meshi or Shari)

Here we provide the directions for making sushi rice on the stove top, but investing in an automatic rice cooker is also a good idea. A rice cooker makes cooking rice easier, and some machines even sense the dryness of the rice that is being cooked and automatically adjust the cooking time using fuzzy logic.

Learning to make good sushi rice takes years of practice and involves everything from deciding on the water you use (filtered or spring is preferred) to how you wash the rice (with vigor or very gently). If you are opening a sushi restaurant, you should consider these things. If not, most tap water is fine and a gentle hand for rinsing is best. When adding the water for cooking the rice, start with the amount we have listed. Once the rice is cooked, check to see if it is a bit too wet or too dry. As rice gets older, it becomes drier, so if your rice has been on the shelf for a while, you may need another 1 or 2 tbsp water. When it is younger and fresher, it needs less water than the amount indicated.

Be sure to use Japanese-style short-grain white rice (*Oryzo sativa* var. *japonica*). Other short-grain types will not work properly.

When you add the vinegar to the rice, the spatula should be kept at a 45-degree angle—a bit like slicing at an angle. As you cut, the rice will naturally fall over onto itself, and as you keep cutting and simultaneously turning the bowl, the sushi vinegar will mix evenly into the rice. A hangiri is the best choice for making sushi rice, because the wood absorbs the moisture from the rice so that the rice can absorb the vinegar. If you lack a hangiri, a wide, shallow glass or ceramic bowl can be substituted. Finally, you will need a fan to cool the rice as you turn it.

How to

Make Sushi Rice (Sushi-meshi or Shari)

MAKES 6 CUPS/960 G, ENOUGH FOR 45 TO 50 PIECES NIGIRI OR 12 HOSOMAKI

2 cups/400 g Japanese-style short-grain white rice

2 cups plus 2 tbsp/510 ml water, preferably filtered or spring

⅓ cup/80 ml sushi vinegar (see page 111)

Put the rice in a medium bowl about 16 in/40 cm in diameter and add enough tap water to cover the rice by 2 to 3 in/ 5 to 7.5 cm. Using your fingers, gently whisk the rice in about five circular motions. As you work, you will see the water become cloudy. Drain the rice, return it to the bowl, add the same amount of water, whisk the rice, and drain again. Repeat this process until the rinsing water is almost clear. For most rice this takes about five rinses.

Drain the rice in a colander and leave it in the colander for 30 minutes. Then transfer the rice to a heavy, medium saucepan about 8 in/20 cm in diameter and 5 in/12 cm deep, with a tight lid. Add the 2 cups plus 2 tbsp/510 ml water and put the lid on the pan,

making sure it is tightly sealed. Place over high heat and heat until you see a steady stream of steam rising from under the lid. Reduce the heat to very low and cook for 13 minutes. Remove from the heat and let stand, covered, for 5 minutes. This final 5 minutes helps to balance the moisture in the rice.

Transfer the rice to a hangiri or a shallow, wide, nonreactive bowl, preferably about 18 in/46 cm in diameter. Using a wooden or silicone spatula moistened with water, gently spread the rice as thinly as possible. Splash the vinegar evenly over the rice (1), then, using the spatula, gently "cut" the rice without smashing the individual grains to mix in the vinegar. The rice must be hot to absorb the vinegar. As you mix the rice and vinegar, use a hand fan to help cool the rice and to remove some moisture (2). If you are coordinated, you should fan and mix the rice at the same time. If you find that too difficult, alternate between mixing and fanning. You want to cool the rice as quickly as possible to body temperature to rid it of extra moisture.

Place a dampened kitchen towel over the rice and keep it as close to body temperature as possible until using. If you cannot use it right away, place it in a warm spot in your kitchen, or keep it warm over the very low heat of a pilot light or double boiler.

Note: If you are making the rice for the sushi bowl recipes that begin on page 206, increase the amount of raw rice to 2½ cups/ 500 g and the water to 2½ cups plus 2½ tbsp/640 ml.

1

2

How to

Make Sushi Rice Balls

This is the basic technique for making the rice balls used for gunkan-maki and for inari-zushi, which is included in the chapter on sushi bowls (see page 216). Directions for making traditional nigiri-zushi appear on page 124. When you are making the rice balls for any of these styles, it is okay to make the rice balls first, then complete the gunkan-maki or inari last. The nori will stay crisper. If you need to make the rice balls up to an hour ahead of time, cover them with plastic wrap but do not refrigerate. You can keep them longer, but the rice will gradually lose its flexibility and stickiness and the balls will be more difficult to top with fish. Once you have added the fish, the sushi should sit for no more than 15 minutes before serving. Any longer and freshness will be lost.

MAKES 4 BALLS

Hand water (see page 113)

½ cup/80 g sushi rice (see page 105) at body temperature, covered with a damp kitchen towel

Moisten the palm side of one hand lightly with hand water, then rub your hands together to moisten them. (Remoisten your hands as necessary to keep the rice from sticking to your hands.) Be careful, however, as too much water will cause the rice to lose its stickiness. These directions are written for a right-handed person. If you are left-handed, reverse the references.

Using your right hand, pick up one-fourth of the rice (about ¾ oz/20 g) and make an egg-shaped ball within your palm (1),

compressing gently but not crushing the rice, and using your fingers to turn the ball in your palm a couple of times. Cup your left hand and place the ball between the second and third joints of the fingers on your left hand. With your left thumb, gently press the center of the rice a bit to introduce some air into it (2). Still holding your thumb on the rice, turn your left hand over so your thumb is supporting the rice ball and the ball is now upside down (3). Now, with the thumb and index finger of your right hand, hold the ball along its length and remove the ball from your left hand (4). Turn your left hand palm-up and quickly place the rice ball back in your left hand along the second and third joints of your fingers, with the center that you pressed facedown (5).

To finish forming the rice ball you need to perform three actions together (6):

1. Allow your left hand to relax naturally and your wrist to bend down, so that the rice ball rests in your cupped fingers.

2. Use the thumb of your left hand to hold and press the end of the rice ball.

3. With the index finger of your right hand, press down gently on the top of the rice ball.

All three actions are done simultaneously in a quick, gentle pressing motion. Then, with your right hand, use your index and middle fingers on one side and your thumb on the other to pick up the rice ball by its sides and turn it in your left hand 180 degrees (7, 8). Repeat the previous three actions

continued >>>

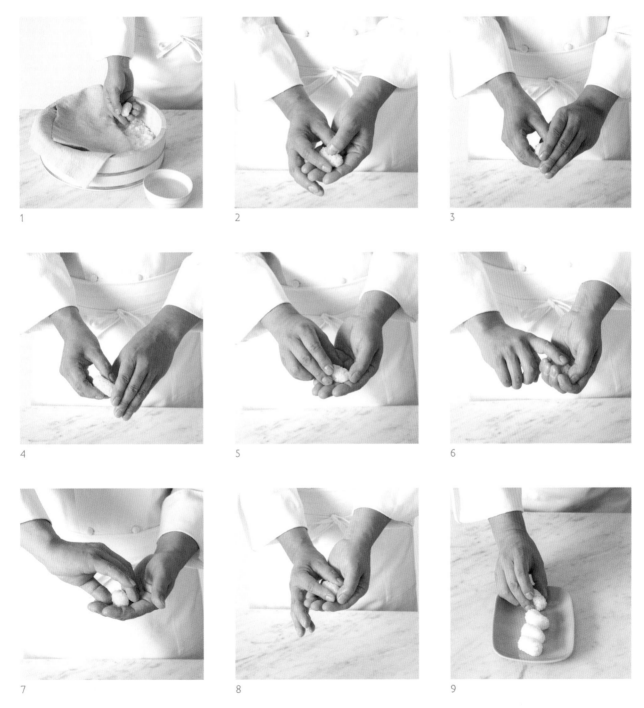

1

2

3

4

5

6

7

8

9

How to

Make Sushi Rice Balls

with the rice ball in this position. You should have a well-shaped sushi rice ball.

Repeat the steps to make three more rice balls.

When you have finished the balls (9), go to the recipe in which you will be using the rice ball to complete the sushi.

How to

Make Sushi Vinegar (Sushi-zu)

This simple concoction is what turns cooked short-grain white rice into sushi rice. Once the seasoned vinegar has been mixed into the rice, the rice is called *sushi-meshi*, *su-meshi*, or *shari*. Each chef has his or her own special balance of seasoning. Many chefs use an esoteric vinegar or more than one kind of vinegar as their trade secret. If possible, make the seasoned vinegar the day before you want to use it. When left to stand overnight, the flavor mellows and is more mature. We suggest using the seasoned vinegar within 3 weeks. After that, it begins to lose its flavor.

MAKES ABOUT 1⅓ CUPS/320 ML

**1 piece kelp for dashi, about
2 in/5 cm square**

1 cup/240 ml rice vinegar

½ cup/100 g sugar

5 tbsp/50 g kosher salt

If you see some dust on the kelp, wipe it off lightly with a paper towel. Do not rinse off the powdery white coating, however, as it carries flavor. In a small saucepan, combine the kelp, vinegar, sugar, and salt; place over medium heat; and bring just to a boil, stirring occasionally to dissolve the sugar and salt. Remove from the heat and let cool to room temperature. Discard the kelp and store the seasoned vinegar in a nonreactive airtight jar in the refrigerator until using.

How to

Toast Nori

Toasting the nori you will be using for sushi is an important step because it crisps it, ensuring a better texture and giving it a rounder, more developed flavor. You can buy already-toasted nori, known as *yaki-nori*, but even yaki-nori is better if you toast it before you use it.

Nori comes in a few different sizes. The size we recommend is a sheet measuring about 8½ by 7½ in/21.5 by 19 cm. Different uses of toasted nori require different-size pieces: sometimes a whole sheet, sometimes a half sheet, sometimes strips.

Turn on a stove-top gas burner to medium-high. Using your fingers, hold the nori sheet about 2 in/5 cm above the flame and pass it over the flame two or three times to toast it evenly. Turn it to toast both sides. The sheet should be very lightly toasted, with no evidence of any blisters or darkening. (If you have an electric stove, use the same technique, holding the sheet about 2 in/5 cm above the burner.) The nori should constrict a bit and become just a little crispier. Set aside until ready to use.

To cut a nori sheet to the size called for in a recipe, use a very sharp knife and cut straight down, or use kitchen scissors. Do not try to cut the nori sheet with a back-and-forth slicing action or it will tear.

How to

Make Hand Water (Tezu)

Tezu is the liquid used to moisten your hands or the blade of your knife when working with sushi rice. By lightly moistening your hands or knife with the liquid, you create a nonstick surface to counteract the stickiness of the rice. As when making sushi rice, it is best to use filtered or spring water so that no off flavors from tap water are introduced.

To make the hand water, in a small bowl, mix together 1 cup/240 ml water and 2 tbsp rice vinegar.

How to
Make Dashi

Dashi is the typical Japanese stock and a staple of Japanese cooking, used for everything from soup bases, stews, and tempura sauce to noodle broth. You need just two ingredients to make it: *dashi kombu*, a type of kelp, and *kezuri-bushi*, or flakes of dried bonito. Do not be tempted to remove the powdery white surface on the kombu, as it is the crystallization of natural glutamates that deliver umami. If you see some dust on the kelp, wipe it off lightly with a paper towel before use.

MAKES ABOUT 2 CUPS/480 ML

2¼ cups/540 ml water, preferably filtered or spring

1 piece kelp for dashi, 3 by 2 in/ 7.5 by 5 cm

⅜ oz/10 g dried bonito shavings

In a small saucepan, combine the water and kelp, place over medium heat, and heat to 148°F/64°C. Hold at this temperature for 10 minutes. Remove the kelp (see Note), heat the liquid to 194°F/90°C, and add the bonito shavings a little at a time so that they do not form lumps. Remove the saucepan from the heat and let rest for 2 minutes.

Line a fine-mesh sieve with a double layer of cheesecloth or a single layer of cloth napkin, place over a nonreactive container, and strain the liquid into the container. Do not press against the solids; instead, let the liquid drip naturally. Let cool completely, cover, and leave at room temperature until ready to use. If you are unable to use the stock the same day, store it in the refrigerator for no more than 1 day.

Note: It is best to buy whole dried bonito fillets and shave them into flakes yourself, but outside of Japan, it is difficult to find whole dried fillets. You can find dried bonito shavings in Japanese markets and well-stocked U.S. supermarkets. When shopping for this recipe, look for a package (sometimes labeled *kezuri-katsuo*) with large, light pink flakes, rather than yellowish-beige flakes.

For the best flavor, make a small amount of dashi and use it the same day, as it starts to lose its flavor within 24 hours. You can refrigerate it, but try to use it within a day for better quality.

After you have made the dashi, the dashi kombu can be preserved (see below) and used in a different way. It is delicious in inari-zushi (see page 216): Chop the preserved dashi kombu and mix it into the sushi rice before placing it in the inari. Or, sprinkle the chopped preserved kombu over chirashi-zushi (see page 212). It is also delicious added to a green salad or to sunomono.

To preserve the leftover dashi kombu, first finely julienne it. Then, in a small saucepan, combine dashi, soy sauce, and mirin in a ratio of four to one to one, add the julienned dashi kombu, and simmer until almost all the liquid has evaporated. Let cool and store in a covered jar in the refrigerator. It will keep for up to 1 month.

How to
Make Vegetarian Dashi

As with nonvegetarian dashi, it is best to make only a small amount and use it the same day to avoid loss of flavor. If you don't use it all, the leftover stock can be refrigerated in an airtight container for up to 1 day. If your kelp is a bit dusty, wipe it gently with a paper towel before use. Do not wipe away the powdery white surface, however. It adds umami.

MAKES 2¼ CUPS/540 ML

2¼ cups/540 ml water, preferably filtered or spring

1 piece kelp for dashi, 3 by 2 in/ 7.5 by 5 cm

Put the water and kelp in a glass jar, cover the jar, and leave the jar at room temperature overnight. Remove the kelp and strain the liquid through a fine-mesh sieve into a nonreactive container to remove any residue left by the kelp. Cover and leave at room temperature until using. (See the note on the facing page for ways to use the leftover kelp.)

This is best the day it is prepared, but can be refrigerated for up to 3 days.

Dashi-flavored Rolled Omelet (Dashi-maki Tamago)

A favorite food of nearly every Japanese child, *dashi-maki tamago* is usually served at room temperature at sushi bars. Some sushi connoisseurs insist that they can judge how good a sushi chef is by the quality of the dashi-maki tamago. In Japan, the best omelets are made with eggs from *jidori*, or cage-free chickens, which have dark, rich yolks. Traditionally, a special rectangular pan is used for cooking the omelet (see page 38). A regular round skillet about 6 in/15 cm in diameter can be substituted.

4 large eggs, preferably from cage-free chickens

¼ cup/60 ml dashi (see page 114)

2 tsp light soy sauce

2 tsp sugar

Vegetable oil for cooking

In a medium bowl, combine the eggs, dashi, soy sauce, and sugar and mix together with chopsticks or a fork. For this recipe, you want to "cut" the eggs, not whip them, as you do not want to add any air. Also, you do not need to mix them thoroughly. It is fine if some unincorporated egg white is visible here and there.

Heat the omelet pan over medium-low heat. Fold a paper towel into a 2-in/5-cm square and dip it into a little vegetable oil. Use the towel to lightly coat the bottom and sides of the pan with oil.

Slowly pour about one-fourth of the egg mixture into the pan and then tilt and swirl the pan to coat the bottom evenly. Using chopsticks, scramble the mixture as if you are making lightly cooked scrambled eggs. Be careful not to overcook the egg mixture; the edges should be a bit dry but the center should look wet. Tilt the pan upward toward you and use a silicone spatula to flip and roll the egg sheet toward you, creating a log shape. Working quickly, swab the exposed part of the pan with the oil-soaked paper towel, push the log to the edge of the pan farthest from you and swab the part of the pan that is now exposed. Pour another one-fourth of the egg mixture into the pan and again tilt and swirl the pan so that the egg mixture evenly covers the bottom of the pan. Gently lift the egg log and allow some of the egg mixture to flow under the log. This will attach the egg log to the new egg sheet.

Once the sheet is just barely set, slightly tilt the pan so that the log is at the top of the pan and start to roll the egg log toward you. Oil the exposed part of pan, push this now-larger egg log to the front end of the pan again, and oil the rest of the pan. Pour one-third of the remaining egg mixture into the pan and repeat the cooking and rolling steps. Repeat two more times with the rest of the egg mixture in two batches. After the final egg layer has been rolled, use the spatula to neaten up the shape of the log against the edge of the pan. You should end up with a brick-shaped omelet about 2½ by 1 by 5 in/6 by 2.5 by 12 cm.

Transfer the finished egg log onto a bamboo sushi mat, roll the mat around the log, and press gently to create a neat brick shape as the egg cools. Balance the roll in the mat on the rim of a soup bowl (select a bowl slightly narrower than the mat) so the air will circulate around the omelet, ensuring it will cool quickly. A small amount of liquid should seep out. If no liquid comes out, the egg roll is overcooked. The omelet can still be used, but keep this in mind when you cook your next omelet, and shorten the cooking time or lower the heat.

Once the omelet is cool, you can leave it resting in the bamboo mat on the countertop if you will be using it within 2 hours. It will be more tender if it has not been chilled. But if you must keep it longer, remove it from the mat, wrap it in plastic wrap, and refrigerate until ready to use. It will keep for up to 2 days. Bring to room temperature before serving.

How to
Make Soy Glaze (Tsume)

This delicious glaze is painted over different preparations of fish for sushi. It is also used to accompany other dishes, such as some vegetarian sushi, or for drizzling over a sushi roll and plate as decoration. The flavor boasts a richness and a delicate sweetness from the dashi and soy sauce, a quality we like to use as an accent in dishes.

MAKES ABOUT ¼ CUP/60 ML

¼ cup/60 ml dashi (see page 114)

2 tbsp soy sauce

1 tbsp sake

1 tbsp mirin

1½ tbsp sugar

½ tsp cornstarch

Pinch of peeled and grated fresh ginger

Pinch of grated garlic

In a small saucepan, combine the dashi, soy sauce, sake, mirin, sugar, cornstarch, ginger, and garlic and stir to combine. Place over medium-high heat and bring to a boil, stirring with a wooden spatula. Simmer until the sauce is reduced to about ¼ cup/60 ml and is the consistency of a thick glaze reminiscent of maple syrup, about 5 minutes.

Pour into a small, heat-proof jar and let cool completely, then cover and refrigerate for up to 2 weeks. Bring to room temperature before using.

How to

Make Ponzu (Soy-Citrus) Sauce

A master ingredient, *ponzu* is wonderfully versatile. In the case of sushi, it is brushed on the fish or served on the side as a sauce. But you can also mix it with a little olive oil to make a great salad dressing, or use it to baste fish before or after grilling or roasting. Mixed with mayonnaise, it is a great dip for vegetables and for fried fish; with the addition of mustard or horseradish, it is the perfect dip for cold crab or lobster.

MAKES ABOUT 1¼ CUPS/300 ML

½ cup/120 ml rice vinegar

6 tbsp/90 ml soy sauce

2 tbsp mirin

Zest of ½ yuzu or lemon, in wide strips

¼ cup/60 ml fresh or bottled yuzu juice or fresh lemon juice

Have ready a medium bowl of ice water. In a small nonreactive saucepan, combine the vinegar, soy sauce, and mirin; place over medium-high heat; and bring to a boil. Remove from the heat, add the yuzu zest, and place the pan in the ice water to cool completely.

Add the yuzu juice and stir to mix. Transfer to a covered container and refrigerate for up to 1 week. Remove the zest before using.

How to

Make Pickled Ginger (Gari)

For this recipe, you will need to buy young ginger, which can be found in most Asian markets. Young ginger has thin, very pale yellow skin, sometimes with a pink blush, and is not as fibrous or as spicy-hot as more mature ginger. The easiest way to peel ginger, young or older, is with a spoon. The skin is thin enough that if you scrape the edge of the spoon over the skin, it takes off all that needs to be removed. This leaves you with much more ginger than if you use a peeler or a knife.

**MAKES ABOUT 1½ CUPS/300 G
DRAINED PICKLED GINGER**

1 lb/455 g fresh young ginger

1½ cups/360 ml rice vinegar

½ cup/120 ml mirin

½ cup/120 ml water

½ cup/100 g sugar

2 tsp kosher salt

Peel the ginger, then, using a Japanese vegetable slicer or a mandoline (or a sharp slicing knife if you have neither), cut lengthwise into slices ¹⁄₁₆ in/ 1.5 mm thick. In a medium bowl, soak the ginger slices in cold water to cover for 30 minutes, then drain.

Bring a large pot filled with water to a boil over high heat. Add the ginger and blanch for 5 seconds, then drain immediately into a colander. Spread the ginger in the colander to cool completely.

Once the slices are cool, squeeze them to remove all the excess liquid. Select a heat-proof 1-qt/ 1-L jar with a tight-fitting lid and put the ginger in it.

In a medium nonreactive sauce-pan, combine the vinegar, mirin, water, sugar, and salt; place over medium heat; and bring just to a boil, stirring occasionally to dissolve the sugar and salt. Pour the hot mixture over the ginger in the jar. Cover the jar with the lid and let cool to room temperature. Refrigerate the ginger overnight before serving. The ginger will keep in the refrigerator for up to 1 month.

How to

Make Spicy Grated Daikon (Momiji Oroshi)

The name of this sushi condiment—*momiji* means "maple" and *oroshi* means "grated"—refers to its color: once the daikon is grated, it is mixed with red pepper that gives it the color of maple leaves in autumn. Momiji oroshi can be stored in a covered container in the refrigerator. That said, we warn you that every time you open the refrigerator door, you will wonder what that smell is. In this case, the smell is much stronger than the taste.

MAKES ABOUT ⅓ CUP/80 ML

One 8-oz/225-g daikon

Pinch of cayenne pepper

¼ tsp paprika

⅛ tsp fresh lemon juice

Peel the daikon, then grate it on a Japanese grater, or cut it into small pieces, put them into a blender, and process until just before they become a purée. (You may need to add 1 tbsp water to get things moving.) Or, grate the daikon on the finest holes on a box grater-shredder.

Scoop the grated daikon into a fine-mesh sieve placed over a bowl and leave to drip for 5 minutes. Do not press against the daikon to release the moisture. Transfer the daikon to a small bowl; add the cayenne, paprika, and lemon juice; and whisk together. Cover and refrigerate for up to 2 days.

Hand-Formed Sushi

(Nigiri-zushi)

Make Nigiri-zushi (Hand-formed Sushi)

This is the basic technique for forming the rice ball and adding the *neta* (topping) to it for traditional nigiri-zushi. This method is used throughout this chapter for many of the fish and for some vegetables.

Have your fish ready to go and kept cold. A good way to do this is to fill a large, shallow bowl with ice and cover the bowl with plastic wrap. As you cut your fish, lay the slices, slightly overlapping, on the plastic wrap over the ice. When you have finished cutting the fish, cover it with plastic wrap, set the bowl to the side, and start making your first rice ball. Finish the first piece of nigiri—shape the ball and top it with the fish—before starting another one. Being organized and having an easily accessible plate or wooden board for the finished sushi will make the operation go more smoothly. Once you develop a rhythm for forming nigiri, you will do it naturally. Until then, just keep practicing.

Hand water (see page 113)

½ cup/80 g sushi rice (see page 105) at body temperature, covered with a damp kitchen towel

4 slices sashimi-grade fish, each 3 by 1 by ¼ in/7.5 cm by 2.5 cm by 6 mm or as specified in individual recipes

Wasabi, as specified in individual recipes

Moisten the palm of one hand lightly with hand water, then rub your hands together. (Remoisten your hands as necessary while making the rice balls to keep the rice from sticking to your hands.) Be careful, however, as too much water will cause the rice to lose its stickiness. The directions are written for a right-handed person. If you are left-handed, reverse them.

Using your right hand, pick up one-fourth of the rice (about ¾ oz/20 g) and make an egg-shaped ball within your palm, compressing gently but not crushing the rice, and using your fingers to turn the ball in your palm a couple of times. Pick up

a fish slice with your left hand, using only your thumb and index finger. Then, with your left hand palm-side up, let the fish rest between the second and third joints of your fingers (1). While holding the shaped sushi rice in your right palm, scoop up a small amount of grated wasabi with the index finger of your right hand and smear the wasabi along the center of the length of the fish (2).

Bring your right hand over the top of your left and place the rice lengthwise on top of the length-wise fish slice (3). At this point, the sushi will be upside down. Cup the sushi in your hand with your fingers and, using the thumb of your left hand, gently press the center of the rice a bit to introduce some air into it (4). Still holding your thumb on the rice, turn your left hand over so your thumb is supporting the rice ball and the sushi is now fish-side up (5). Then, with your right-hand thumb and index finger (6), hold the rice along the length of the nigiri and quickly place it, fish-side up, back across the middle joints of your left hand (7).

To finish forming the rice ball, you need to perform three actions together (8):

1. Allow your left hand to relax naturally and your wrist to bend down, so that the nigiri rests in the cupped position of your fingers.

2. Use the thumb of your left hand to hold and press the end of the rice ball.

3. Hold the index and middle fingers of your right hand together and straight and press down gently on the top of the fish.

All three actions are done simultaneously in a quick, gentle pressing motion. Then, with your right hand, use your index and middle fingers on one side and your thumb on the other to pick up the sushi by its sides and turn it in your left hand 180 degrees (9). Repeat the previous three actions with the sushi in this position. You should have a well-shaped piece of nigiri. If you feel it needs a little more work, turn it 180 degrees and repeat the three actions (10).

Place the finished nigiri on a serving plate or wooden board (11). Repeat the steps to make three more nigiri. Serve as directed in individual recipes.

How to

Make Nigiri-zushi (Hand-formed Sushi)

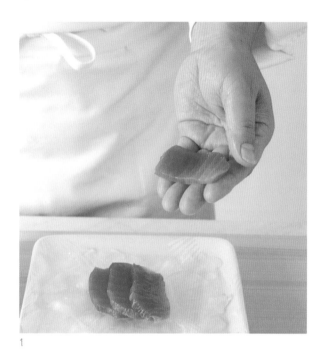

1

2   >>>

5

6

3

4

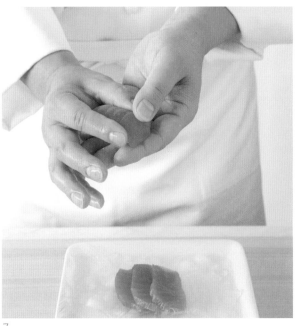

7

8

How to
Make Nigiri-zushi
(Hand-formed Sushi)

9

10

11

Nigiri with Albacore (Binchomaguro/Tombo)

Also known as *tombo*, *binnaga*, *bincho*, longfin tuna, and white tuna, albacore is a type of tuna with almost-white flesh. In Japanese, the same ideograms, meaning "long sideburns," are used for both *bincho* and *binnaga*. The albacore was so named during the shogun era because the fish reminded folks of a face framed by long sideburns when viewed from the front. *Longfin* comes from the extreme length of the pectoral fin of the albacore, which is some-times as much as half its total length. Line-caught fresh albacore in season is one of our favorite fish. It has a silky texture and nice fat in every bite, tasting almost like *toro*, the fattiest cut of tuna. Although albacore is available in sashimi grade, it is mostly found frozen because the local season is short.

Following the directions for How to Make Nigiri-zushi (page 124), make 4 nigiri with the rice, fish, and wasabi. Serve with soy sauce for dipping.

½ cup/80 g sushi rice (see page 105) at body temperature, covered with a damp kitchen towel

4 slices albacore, each 3 by 1¼ by ⅜ in/7.5 by 3 by 1 cm (see How to Slice Tuna for Nigiri, page 81)

¼ tsp wasabi

Soy sauce for serving

Nigiri with Tuna (Maguro)

This is the first sushi most people try at a sushi bar and at home, and because of that, it is often taken for granted later. The difference between a tuna nigiri made with great tuna and a tuna nigiri in an assortment of prepackaged sushi at the supermarket is like night and day. If you are starting with a whole tuna and filleting it yourself, see How to Break Down Bonito on page 75. If not, look for a high-quality sashimi-grade tuna steak in an upscale grocery store or fish market. Tuna nigiri is the perfect nigiri to start with, because tuna has a firm texture and is easy to cut and form. Different parts of the tuna fillet have different textures. The back loin pieces are firmer, less fatty, and simple to work with. The belly side of the fish is fattier and also has more sinew, which makes it a little more difficult to cut. It is nice to have both kinds on a sushi plate.

½ cup/80 g sushi rice (see page 105) at body temperature, covered with a damp kitchen towel

4 slices tuna loin, each 3 by 1¼ by ⅜ in/7.5 by 3 by 1 cm (see How to Slice Tuna for Nigiri, page 81, if starting with a steak or large loin; if not, see How to Slice Bonito for Nigiri, page 80)

¼ tsp wasabi

Soy sauce for serving

Following the directions for How to Make Nigiri-zushi (page 124), make 4 nigiri with the rice, tuna, and wasabi. Serve with soy sauce.

Nigiri with Soy-marinated Tuna (Maguro no zuke)

Zuke means "marinated" or "cured" in Japanese. Every sushi chef has his or her own recipe for zuke, or seasoned soy sauce, and no two are exactly the same. We bring a bit of California to this nigiri with the addition of jalapeño chile and avocado, for a perfect pairing. The presence of the jalapeño means that you don't need to serve wasabi on the side. This sushi does not require soy sauce for serving.

SOY MARINADE (ZUKE)

1½ tsp sake

1½ tsp mirin

1 tbsp dashi (see page 114)

1 tbsp dark soy sauce

4 jalapeño chile slices, each ⅛ in/3 mm thick, seeded

4 slices tuna loin, each 3 by 1¼ by ⅜ in/7.5 by 3 by 1 cm (see How to Slice Tuna for Nigiri, page 81, if starting with a steak or large loin; if not, see How to Slice Bonito for Nigiri, page 80)

½ cup/80 g sushi rice (see page 105) at body temperature, covered with a damp kitchen towel

¼ tsp wasabi

⅛ Hass avocado, peeled and cut crosswise into 16 slices, each ⅛ in/3 mm

8 vinegar-cured small capers, rinsed and patted dry

To make the soy marinade: Have ready a medium-size bowl filled with ice water. In a small sauce-pan, combine the sake and mirin and bring just to a boil over high heat. Remove from the heat, pour into a small heat-proof bowl, and place the bowl in the ice water to cool. Once the mixture is cool, add the dashi and soy sauce and pour the marinade into a small, shallow container just large enough to hold the tuna slices in a single layer.

Add the jalapeño slices to the marinade and marinate for 30 minutes, then remove from the marinade and pat dry. Add the tuna slices to the marinade and marinate for 2 minutes, then remove the tuna slices from the marinade and pat dry.

Following the directions for How to Make Nigiri-zushi (page 124), make 4 nigiri with the rice, tuna, and wasabi. Place the nigiri on a serving plate. Garnish each nigiri with 4 avocado slices, and place a jalapeño slice on the center of the nigiri. Top each jalapeño slice with 2 capers and serve.

Nigiri with West Coast King Salmon (Sake)

Many different salmon species exist, but in our opinion, king salmon is definitely the king of them all. It has a fat content and a silky texture that makes it one of the most popular fish in sushi bars. We use only wild salmon in season, a rare treat that reminds us each time the season returns why we like this fish so much. If you are fortunate enough to find a whole one, see How to Break Down Round Fish on page 54. Salmon is known to carry parasites (especially farmed specimens raised in crowded conditions, which you should avoid in any case), and certain safety measures are advised before serving it raw (see sidebar).

Following the directions for How to Make Nigiri-zushi (page 124), make 4 nigiri with the rice, salmon, and wasabi. Serve with soy sauce.

½ cup/80 g sushi rice (see page 105) at body temperature, covered with a damp kitchen towel

4 slices salmon fillet, each 3 by 1¼ by ⅜ in/7.5 by 3 by 1 cm (see How to Slice Round Fish Fillet for Nigiri, page 64)

¼ tsp wasabi

Soy sauce for serving

Raw Salmon Precaution

Because salmon often carries parasites, the U.S. Food and Drug Administration (FDA) recommends that you freeze raw salmon to kill any parasites before serving it as sushi or sashimi. According to the FDA, raw fresh salmon should be handled in one of the following ways:

- Freeze and store at −4°F/ −20°C or below for 7 days (total time); or

- Freeze at −31°F/−35°C or below until solid and store at −31°F/−35°C or below for 15 hours; or

- Freeze at −31°F/−35°C or below until solid and store at −4°F/−20°C or below for 24 hours.

Nigiri with California Halibut (Hirame)

The California halibut is much smaller than the Alaskan halibut. We prefer buying the whole fish, which weighs about 4 lb/1.8 kg, for preparing this sushi, rather than starting with a purchased fillet. At that size, the flesh is more delicate. Choose a fish that is firm to the touch, has a clean ocean smell, and is coated with a thin slimy substance that acts as a protection. See page 43 for directions on How to Break Down Flatfish (see Note). This sushi does not require soy sauce or wasabi for serving.

½ cup/80 g sushi rice (see page 105) at body temperature, covered with a damp kitchen towel

4 slices California halibut fillet, each 3 by 1 by ¼ in/7.5 cm by 2.5 cm by 6 mm (see How to Slice Flatfish Fillet for Nigiri, page 51)

½ shiso leaf, cut crosswise into 4 equal strips

Sea salt

½ Meyer lemon

Following the directions for How to Make Nigiri-zushi (page 124), make 4 nigiri with the rice and fish, laying a shiso strip length-wise on the rice (and omitting the wasabi). The green of the shiso should be slightly visible through the translucent fish slice. Once the nigiri are on a serving plate, sprinkle a tiny pinch of sea salt over each fish slice, top with a small squeeze of lemon juice, and serve.

Note: If you start with a whole halibut, save the fin muscles that run around the edge of the fish. In Japanese, this part of the halibut is called the *engawa*, or "corridor." English does not really have a word for this part of the fish, and, unfortunately, in America it is usually thrown away. The texture of engawa is firmer and crunchier than the fillet. You can garnish it in the same way the fillet slices are garnished here, or you can put a ¼-tsp-size ball of spicy grated daikon (see page 121) in the center of the fish, sprinkle with a little chopped fresh chive, and finish with a splash of ponzu sauce (see page 119).

Nigiri with California Halibut Aspic (Hirame no Nikogori)

This recipe will make enough halibut aspic (*nikogori*) for ten nigiri, but you can make just four nigiri and freeze the leftover nikogori for up to a month. If you do freeze it, you will need to warm it in a small pan until melted and then reset it as instructed in the recipe. Since the fish fins, bones, and skin have so much natural gelatin, the aspic will reset easily. We like this recipe because it tastes good and adds another dimension of texture to sushi but also because it gives you something to do with the bones so they are not wasted. This sushi does not require soy sauce for serving.

Bones, fins, and skin from one 4-lb/1.8-kg halibut (see How to Break Down Flatfish, page 43)

8 qt/7.5 L tap water

6 cups/1.4 L filtered or spring water

2 tbsp soy sauce

2 tbsp sugar

¼ tsp peeled and grated fresh ginger

½ cup/80 g sushi rice (see page 105) at body temperature, covered with a damp kitchen towel

¼ tsp wasabi

Soak the bones, fins, and skin under a fine trickle of cold running water for 1 hour, then drain.

In a large saucepan, bring the 8 qt/7.5 L tap water to a boil over high heat. Add the bones, fins, and skin and blanch for 1 minute, then drain into a sieve. Return the bones and fins to the pan and reserve the skin. Add the 6 cups/1.4 L filtered water, soy sauce, sugar, and ginger to the pan and bring to a boil over high heat. Lower the heat to a simmer and skim off any impurities that rise to the surface. Simmer, uncovered, for about 40 minutes, until the joints between the bones melt and the bones separate.

Remove from the heat and strain through a fine-mesh sieve. Discard the bones and fins. Clean the pan, return the strained stock to it, and bring to a simmer. Cut the fish skin into strips about ¼ by 1½ in/6 mm by 4 cm. Add the skin strips to the saucepan and simmer gently, skimming any impurities that rise to the surface, until the liquid is reduced by one-third, about 1 hour. You should have about 1 cup/240 ml.

Line the bottom and sides of a 5-by-6-in/12-by-15-cm sheet pan with plastic wrap, and pour the liquid and skin into the pan. The liquid should be ⅜ in/1 cm deep. Put the pan, uncovered, in the refrigerator to set. Once firmly set, remove the pan from the refrigerator. Place a small cutting board over the sheet pan and carefully and gently flip the board and pan together. Lift off the pan and peel off the plastic wrap.

Cut the aspic into 10 slices, each 3 by 1 in/7.5 by 2.5 cm. Arrange the slices on a plate, cover, and refrigerate until ready to use. To make this recipe, set aside 4 slices, and then freeze the remainder (see headnote).

Following the directions for How to Make Sushi Rice Balls (page 108), make 4 rice balls and place them on a serving plate. Smear a little of the wasabi on the top of each rice ball, drape an aspic slice over the each ball, and serve.

Note: Because this sushi is based on natural gelatin, make this nigiri last if you are assembling an assortment of sushi. The aspic should stay as cold as possible before serving.

Nigiri with Sea Bass (Suzuki)

In California in the summertime, you can find amazing sea bass, labeled California white bass, in the fish markets. If you are on the East Coast, wild-caught striped bass is a great choice. Both of these fish have a mild flavor and slightly firm flesh. You want to use the fillet from a fish that weighs 3 to 6 lb/1.4 to 2.7 kg, as the flesh will have a mature flavor but still have a delicate texture ideal for sushi.

½ cup/80 g sushi rice (see page 105) at body temperature, covered with a damp kitchen towel

4 slices sea bass, about 3 by 1 by ¼ in/7.5 cm by 2.5 cm by 6 mm (see How to Break Down Round Fish, page 54)

¼ tsp wasabi

Soy sauce for serving

Following the directions for How to Make Nigiri-zushi (page 124), make 4 nigiri with the rice, fish, and wasabi. Serve with soy sauce.

Nigiri with Kombu-cured Big Island Amberjack (Kanpachi no Kombu-jime)

MAKES 4 NIGIRI

Kanpachi, a type of amberjack related to the yellowtail jack, is farmed successfully on the Big Island of Hawaii, where sustainable practices make it a good choice over farm-raised yellowtail jack (*hamachi*). For the best flavor, be sure to allow the amberjack to cure in the *kombu* (kelp) sheets overnight. Then remove the fish from the kombu and use it the same day, or wrap it and refrigerate for up to 1 day before using. If the kombu is thick, it will take a little longer to soften.

2 pieces kelp for dashi, each 4 by 5 in/10 by 12 cm

4 slices amberjack fillet, each 3 by 1½ by ¼ in/7.5 cm by 4 cm by 6 mm (see How to Slice Round Fish Fillet for Nigiri, page 64)

Kosher salt

½ cup/80 g sushi rice (see page 105) at body temperature, covered with a damp kitchen towel

¼ tsp wasabi

¼ shiso leaf, cut crosswise into 4 equal strips

Soy sauce for serving

Lightly wipe the kelp pieces with a moistened clean kitchen towel. Cover with the towel and set aside for 20 minutes. Then check the kelp pieces to see if they are soft. They should be soft enough to flatten out. Place one of the kelp pieces on a plate, and lay the amberjack slices on the kelp in one layer without overlapping. Sprinkle with a little salt, cover the fish slices with the second kelp piece, wrap with plastic wrap, and refrigerate for at least 3 hours if you prefer a light cure or up to 8 hours if you prefer a stronger cure.

Following the directions for How to Make Nigiri-zushi (page 124), make 4 nigiri with the rice, fish, and wasabi. After you smear the wasabi onto the fish slice, place 1 strip of the shiso on the fish, then place the rice onto the shiso and continue making the nigiri as directed. Serve with soy sauce.

Nigiri with Seared Bonito (Katsuo no Tataki)

Bonito tataki is famous in Kochi Prefecture on the Japanese island of Shikoku. *Tataki*, which means "pounded," traditionally calls for quickly searing bonito fillets with skin still attached over an open flame of rice straw. The searing concentrates the taste of the flesh and gives the fish a different texture, plus the smokiness from the burning rice straw contributes to a unique, more complex flavor. After the fish is plated, fresh herbs and condiments are placed on it, a sauce is poured over the toppings and the fish, and the toppings are struck—or pounded—with the flat side of a knife blade to help their flavors penetrate the fish.

This technique has been extended to other types of fish and to meats, as well, and now the word *tataki* is used for a contemporary cooking technique in which fish or meat is seared on the outside and served either raw or very rare on the inside. This sushi does not require soy sauce or wasabi for serving.

1 tbsp vegetable oil

8 slices garlic, each ¹⁄₁₆ in/1.5 mm thick

Kosher salt

4 garlic chives, each about 8 in/20 cm long (see Note)

½ cup/80 g sushi rice (see page 105) at body temperature, covered with a damp kitchen towel

4 slices bonito tataki, each 3 by 1¼ by ⅜ in/7.5 by 3 by 1 cm (see How to Make Seared Bonito, page 78)

¼ tsp peeled and grated fresh ginger

½ tsp ponzu sauce (page 119)

In a small sauté pan, combine the oil and garlic over low heat and cook until the garlic is crisp and light golden brown, about 2 minutes. Using a slotted spoon, transfer the garlic slices to paper towels to remove the excess fat, then season with salt. Set aside.

Have ready a bowl of ice water. Bring a small saucepan filled with water to a boil over high heat and salt the water. Add the garlic chives and blanch for 1 second.

Drain and immediately immerse in the ice water to halt the cooking. Remove from the ice water and pat dry.

Following the directions for How to Make Nigiri-zushi (page 124), make 4 nigiri with the rice and fish and replace the wasabi with the ginger. Tie each nigiri around the middle crosswise with a garlic chive, and arrange the garlic chips on the fish. Sprinkle each nigiri with an equal amount of the ponzu sauce and serve.

Note: You may want to blanch a couple of extra garlic chives. Sometimes when tying them around the sushi, they break.

Nigiri with True Snapper (Madai)

Tai means "snapper" in Japanese, which encompasses many different kinds of fish, and *madai*, or true snapper, is the most prized of the lot, often served for celebrations or given as a gift. We gave a madai to each of the guests at our wedding in Japan. Sometimes labeled red sea bream in English, the fish is hard to find in fish markets in the United States, though good alternatives exist, such as striped bass, barramundi, and the similar red porgy. This sushi is pictured on the top of the facing page.

½ cup/80 g sushi rice (see page 105) at body temperature, covered with a damp kitchen towel

4 slices true snapper fillet, each 3 by 1 by ¼ in/7.5 cm by 2.5 cm by 6 mm thick (see How to Slice Round Fish Fillet for Nigiri, page 64)

¼ tsp wasabi

Soy sauce for serving

Following the directions for How to Make Nigiri-zushi (page 124), make 4 nigiri with the rice, fish, and wasabi. Serve with soy sauce.

Variations: When you fillet the whole snapper, save the liver and soak it in ice water for about 1 hour, then drain. Have ready a medium-size bowl filled with ice water. In a small saucepan, combine dashi (see page 114), soy sauce, and mirin in a ratio of eight to one to one. Add a pinch of peeled and grated fresh ginger and bring to a simmer over medium heat. Add the liver and simmer for 3 minutes, then remove from the heat, pour the contents of the pan into a heat-proof bowl, and place the bowl in the ice water until cool. Then chill the liver well, still in the liquid, in the refrigerator. Remove the liver from the liquid and cut into ½-in/12-mm squares. Place a square of the liver on each snapper nigiri and top with a little chopped fresh chive. The addition of the liver and chive gives the nigiri more depth of flavor.

A second option is to leave the skin attached when you fillet the snapper. Place one fillet, skin-side up, in a colander, sprinkle some kosher salt evenly over the skin, and cover with a thin cloth. Have ready a large bowl filled with ice water. Pour 2 cups/480 ml boiling water in a slow stream over the fillet, then immediately immerse the fillet in the ice water. Let cool completely in the ice water, remove from the water, pat dry, and slice as directed for a skinned fillet. The texture and the richness of the skin give this nigiri another dimension.

Nigiri with Olive Oil-marinated Sardines (Iwashi)

Fresh sardines are abundant and reasonably priced, plus they are a great source of healthful omega-3 fatty acids. Yuzu with pepper—a pastelike condiment made from yuzu peel, salt, and chile—is a zesty complement to fatty, oily fish like sardines. The olive oil masks some of the fishy scent and also marries pleasantly with the sushi rice. We recommend using an extra-virgin olive oil that is not too strongly flavored. This sushi, pictured at bottom on page 141, does not require soy sauce or wasabi for serving.

2 fresh sardines, each about 6 in/15 cm long, filleted (see How to Break Down Sardines, page 93)

¼ tsp kosher salt

¼ tsp fresh lime juice

4 lime slices, each ⅛ in/3 mm thick, plus finely chopped or grated lime zest

1 tbsp extra-virgin olive oil

½ cup/80 g sushi rice (see page 105) at body temperature, covered with a damp kitchen towel

½ tsp yuzu with pepper

4 small fennel sprigs

Place the sardine fillets in a single layer in a shallow, flat nonreactive container, sprinkle the salt evenly over both sides of each fillet, cover, and refrigerate for 30 minutes. Pat the fillets dry with paper towels and return the fillets to the container.

Drizzle the lime juice over the fillets, and place a lime slice on each fillet. Drizzle the olive oil evenly over the fillets, cover with plastic wrap, and marinate in the refrigerator for at least 1 hour or up to 3 hours. Remove the fillets from the marinade, discard the lime sauce, and pat dry with paper towels.

Following the directions for How to Make Nigiri-zushi (page 124), make 4 nigiri with the rice and fish (but without wasabi). Place the nigiri on a serving plate, garnish each sardine with a dot of the yuzu with pepper, and arrange the fennel sprigs on top of the yuzu with pepper. Sprinkle with the lime zest and serve.

Nigiri with Vinegar-cured Mackerel (Shime Saba)

Mackerel, or *saba*, is rich in oil, omega-3 fatty acids, and vitamin E, but because it has what some people define as a fishy scent, it is not popular with everyone. It belongs to the *hikari-mono* ("shiny things") group of fish, part of the blue fish family, which also includes sardines and shads. These fish are generally economical because of their abundance. They are also known to spoil rather quickly, especially mackerel. That's why mackerel is typically cured in salt for at least a couple of hours and then marinated in rice vinegar. Once cured it is called *shime saba*, or "cured mackerel." This sushi does not require soy sauce or wasabi for serving.

Following the directions for How to Make Nigiri-zushi (page 124), make 4 nigiri with the rice and fish (omit the wasabi). Place the nigiri on a serving plate and divide the pickled ginger evenly among the nigiri, placing it on top in the center of the mackerel. Sprinkle the chives evenly over the ginger and serve.

½ cup/80 g sushi rice (see page 105) at body temperature, covered with a damp kitchen towel

4 slices Vinegar-cured Mackerel (page 104), each 3 by 1 by ¼ in/ 7.5 cm by 2.5 cm by 6 mm

1 tsp julienned pickled ginger (see page 120)

1 tsp chopped fresh chives

Nigiri with Poached Shrimp (Ebi)

Whenever you order a nigiri-zushi combination in a restaurant, nigiri with poached shrimp is among the selections. Some people turn up their noses at something so simple. Others relish the uncomplicated flavor of a well-poached shrimp. This recipe not only explains how to prepare a classic nigiri but also provides directions for how to cook shrimp properly for other uses. You can enclose the poached shrimp in sushi rolls, use them in sunomono, or even serve them with a classic American cocktail sauce. For the best flavor, always cook shrimp in their shells, let them cool, and then peel them. The preferred shrimp for sushi are fresh wild shrimp that have been caught sustainably. Another good choice is IQF (individually quick frozen) shrimp in the shell, also from a sustainable source.

MARINADE

2 tbsp rice vinegar

1 tbsp dry sake

1 tbsp sugar

1 tsp kosher salt

⅛ tsp peeled and grated fresh ginger

¼ cup/60 ml water

4 shrimp in the shell without heads, each about 1 oz/30 g (16 to 20 shrimp per 1 lb/455 g)

4 cups/960 ml water

2 tbsp kosher salt

½ cup/80 g sushi rice (see page 105) at body temperature, covered with a damp kitchen towel

¼ tsp wasabi

Soy sauce for serving

To make the marinade: Have ready a medium-size bowl of ice water. In a small nonreactive saucepan, combine the vinegar, sake, sugar, salt, ginger, and water and bring to a boil over high heat. Remove from the heat, pour into a small heat-proof bowl, and place the bowl in the ice water to cool. Transfer the cooled marinade to a container about 5 by 3½ by 2 in/12 by 9 by 5 cm, cover, and refrigerate.

Rinse the shrimp under cold running water. An intestinal tract with impurities runs along the back side of the shrimp body, from the base of the head to the tail. With one hand, hold the shrimp gently from the head to the tail, accentuating the arch

in the back of the shrimp. This will open the shell plates and allow you to see if there is a dark intestinal tract just under the top of the meat. If there is a dark line, this is the intestinal tract and needs to be removed. If it is left in place, it develops a sandy consistency when cooked and is unpleasant to eat. Using a bamboo skewer 6 in/15 cm long, carefully insert the skewer between the second and third shell plates, just under the dark line. Holding the skewer between your thumb and index finger, slowly and gently pull up. The tract should come up to the surface of the shrimp tail. Place your index finger gently on the tract and continue to lift up. Hopefully the entire tract will come out. If not, insert the skewer between the next set of shell plates where you can see the tract and repeat the process until the shrimp is clean. Rinse the shrimp under cold running water. Repeat until all the shrimp are cleaned, then discard the skewer.

Straighten the shrimp, then skewer each shrimp through the middle, starting at the head end and ending at the tail. This will keep the shrimp straight while cooking. In an 8-in-/20-cm-diameter saucepan, bring the 4 cups/960 ml water and the salt to a boil. Have ready a large bowl of ice water.

Immerse the skewered shrimp in the boiling water for 1 minute and transfer to a colander to cool off at room temperature for 5 minutes. Then place the shrimp in the ice water to chill for 2 minutes. Remove from the ice water, pat dry, and remove the skewers. Peel off the shell from each shrimp, leaving the last shell segment and the tail shell still attached to the shrimp. Butterfly each shrimp along the belly side. Make a cut from the head to the tail about three-fourths of the way through, so the shrimp will lie flat like an opened book. Be careful not to cut all the way through. Double-check the interior of the shrimp to make sure no dark tract remains. If some does remain, scrape it off with a small knife, then wipe the shrimp with a moistened towel. Place the cleaned and butterflied shrimp in the marinade for 15 minutes. Remove from the marinade and pat dry.

Following the directions for How to Make Nigiri-zushi (page 124), make 4 nigiri with the rice, shrimp, and wasabi, smearing the wasabi on the cut side of the shrimp and presenting the back side faceup. Serve with soy sauce.

Note: You can poach and marinate the shrimp in advance. Remove from the marinade, cover with plastic wrap, and refrigerate for up to 3 days before making the sushi.

Nigiri with Santa Barbara Spot Prawns (Botan Ebi)

Finding live prawns to buy can be difficult, and one of the best places to look for them is in Asian markets that have a live-fish department. It is also possible to buy spot prawns that were previously frozen and have been thawed. This is what you find at most sushi bars in the United States. If you find them, ask the fishmonger how long they have been thawed. If it is more than a half day, pass them up. Better yet, ask your fishmonger if you can buy them still frozen and then thaw them yourself at home in the refrigerator.

4 Santa Barbara spot prawns, about 4 oz/115 g each, live or frozen and thawed

½ cup/80 g sushi rice (see page 105) at body temperature, covered with a damp kitchen towel

¼ tsp wasabi

Pinch of grated lemon zest

Soy sauce for serving

Rinse the prawns under cold running water. To remove the head from the body, grasp a kitchen towel in each hand to protect your hands (the head of the prawn can prick you and sometimes cause an infection).

Grab the head with your left hand and grab the tail with your right hand (or the reverse if you are left-handed), positioning your left hand as close as possible to the back of the head. With a twisting motion, pull the tail out and disconnect it from the head. Be careful, as the shell is very sharp. The tails will be used for the sushi. (See Note for how the heads can be used.)

Using kitchen scissors, cut the shell from the inside of the prawn along the legs and remove the tail meat. Place the prawn on its side on the cutting board and make a shallow cut along the inside curve of the prawn to butterfly the tail, cutting about three-fourths of the way through the tail. The tail should now rest flat on the cutting board.

Following the directions for How to Make Nigiri-zushi (page 124), make 4 nigiri with the rice, prawns, and wasabi, smearing the wasabi on the cut side of the prawn and presenting the back side faceup. Place the nigiri on a serving plate and sprinkle a small amount of the lemon zest over each nigiri. Serve with soy sauce.

Note: The prawn heads are also edible. Sushi chefs usually deep-fry them and serve them after the sushi. To do this at home, lightly dust the heads with a mixture of equal parts all-purpose flour and cornstarch and deep-fry them in 360°F/185°C vegetable oil until golden and crispy. Accompany them with a wedge of lemon. The heads are also used in a simple, traditional miso soup. The heads release a crustacean flavor into the soup, making it particularly fragrant and delicious.

Nigiri with Sea Scallops (Hotate-gai)

No substitute exists for the sweetness of a live scallop. Unfortunately, live scallops are difficult to find in U.S. markets. The best bets for locating them are in high-end fish markets or at farmers' markets in areas close to the ocean. Like all seafood, a fresh live scallop should have a sweet ocean smell. Because live scallops are so hard to find, we recommend that you substitute sashimi-grade IQF (individually quick frozen) scallops in U-10 size (10 scallops per 1 lb/455 g). Let them thaw in the refrigerator. Scallops are actually the adductor muscle of the shellfish.

2 live scallops, about 1 lb/455 g each, or frozen and thawed cleaned scallops (U-10 size), about 1½ oz/45 g each

½ cup/80 g sushi rice (see page 105) at body temperature, covered with a damp kitchen towel

¼ tsp wasabi

Soy sauce for serving

Rinse the live scallops under cold running water. Place a scallop on the cutting board, flat-side up and with the hinge to the left. (If you are left-handed, reverse the direction of the hinge and equivalent directions elsewhere, and use your left hand to wield the knife throughout the instructions.) Holding the scallop with your left hand, slip a pallet knife (flat, flexible, blunt blade) between the two shells at the end opposite the hinge. Make sure the tip of the knife slides along the bottom of the shell without disturbing the central adductor muscle (which is the scallop itself). Slip the knife into the shell a couple of times, each time changing the entrance location slightly and carefully running under the adductor muscle. This should release the adductor from the shell. Now flip the shell over, and using the same technique, release the adductor from the second shell. Remove the large whitish adductor muscle to a plate, then transfer the remaining parts inside the shell to a bowl. Some of these latter parts we like to eat, such as the *himo*, or "mantle," and the roe (see Note, page 149). Clean them out from the rest of the parts and save them to use, then discard the other parts.

You should be left with just the round cleaned scallop. Rinse it briefly under cold running water, making sure you rinse away any sand, then pat dry. Repeat with the remaining live scallop. If you are using thawed frozen scallops, rinse them briefly under cold running water and pat dry.

Place the scallops on a cutting board and cut each one in half horizontally to yield two rounds. Then butterfly each scallop half by slicing it in half horizontally to within ⅜ in/1 cm of the opposite side so it will lie flat like a book and fit nicely on the rice.

Following the directions for How to Make Nigiri-zushi (page 124), make 4 nigiri with the rice, scallops, and wasabi, placing the scallops cut-side down on the rice. Serve with soy sauce.

Variation: We also like to serve this sea scallop sushi with fresh lemon juice seasoned with a little sea salt instead of soy sauce. The combination lifts the taste of the scallop and intensifies the ocean flavor. So if you are having two pieces, you can enjoy one with soy sauce and the other with lemon and salt to see which taste you prefer.

continued >>>

Note: Japanese love the *himo*, or "mantle," of the scallop, and it is starting to be appreciated in the United States, as well. The himo is the frilly part around the outside edge of the scallop body. It is darker than the body, usually beige to light brown. When you detach it from the other parts in the scallop, it looks a bit like a string (*himo* literally means "string" in Japanese). You can rinse this part and eat it raw as sashimi; it will be quite crunchy. Or, to make it more tender, you can blanch it in boiling salted water for 1 second and then immediately immerse it in ice water. You can chop it into ½-in/12-mm pieces and use it to garnish the scallop nigiri or add it to *sunomono* (vinegared salad).

The roe is also wonderful. You can poach it in salted water heated to about 145°F/62°C for 2 minutes, then remove it from the water, let it cool until it can be handled, and cut it into slices ¼ in/6 mm thick. Use the slices in a gunkan-maki (see page 166). You could also use the himo in a gunkan-maki, or you can mix the roe and the himo together, putting a little roe on one side and a little himo on the other side.

Nigiri with Cherrystone Clams (Hamaguri)

Cherrystone clams are available year-round, usually from the East Coast. Pick ones that feel heavy for their size and have a nice ocean smell. To check for quality, gently tap two clams together. If the clams are fresh and alive, you should hear a high-pitched, dry sound. Also, if a clam does not close tightly when it is tapped, it is probably dead and you should discard it. Always buy an extra clam or two to make sure you have enough healthy ones for your sushi.

4 cherrystone clams

2/3 cup/105 g sushi rice (see page 105) at body temperature, covered with a damp kitchen towel

1/8 tsp wasabi

2 lemon slices, each 1/16 in/2 mm thick, cut into 8 wedges

4 shiso leaves, each halved lengthwise

Soy sauce for serving

Shuck the clams. Separate each clam shell into two shells, rinse, and dry. Reserve the shells for presentation. Slice each clam meat in half horizontally. Pat dry with paper towels.

Follow the directions for How to Make Sushi Rice Balls (page 108), but increase the amount of rice to 2/3 cup/105 g. Divide the rice into eight portions and form each portion into a small ball. Smear a little wasabi on each rice ball and place half of a clam, cut-side down, on each ball. Place a lemon wedge on top of each clam, then wrap a shiso leaf half around each nigiri, making sure the seam of the leaf is on bottom of the nigiri. Place each nigiri in a clam shell. Serve with soy sauce.

Nigiri with Geoduck Clam (Mirugai)

Geoducks are big clams, averaging about 2 lb/960 g each and with a shell length of some 8 in/20 cm. There are two kinds of geoduck: one with dark skin, which sushi chefs call *hon miru* (true mirugai), and one with light skin, which sushi chefs call *shiro miru* (white mirugai). The latter type is more common in U.S. markets. Both types have a sweet, clean ocean taste and pleasantly crunchy texture. Sushi chefs prefer the crunchiness of the siphon part for sushi, reserving the body portion for other uses, such as soup, tempura, sunomono, or sautéed like abalone. In some Asian markets, you may be able to find geoduck clam already cleaned and ready to use to make sushi or sashimi.

Following the directions for How to Make Nigiri-zushi (page 124), make 4 nigiri with the rice, clam, and wasabi. Serve with soy sauce, or with a squeeze of lemon juice and a bit of coarse salt. Try a piece of nigiri each way to see which way you like it best.

½ cup/80 g sushi rice (see page 105) at body temperature, covered with a damp kitchen towel

4 slices geoduck clam, each 3 by 1 by ³⁄₁₆ in/7.5 cm by 2.5 cm by 5 mm (see How to Break Down Geoduck Clam, page 101)

¼ tsp wasabi

Soy sauce or lemon wedge and coarse sea salt for serving

Nigiri with Conger Eel (Anago)

Two types of eel are generally eaten at sushi restaurants: saltwater (*anago*), which is usually simmered and is the lighter flavored of the two, and freshwater (*unagi*), which is typically grilled and is darker and richer. Both types can be purchased already processed, and you can find ready-made eel glaze also. Anago is a bit harder to find but is worth seeking out, as it has a very delicate flavor with a natural light sweetness and an almost firm, creamy texture. If you are able to purchase a whole saltwater eel, you will have the bones and head for making the braising liquid.

Much of this recipe can be done in advance. You can prepare the eel to the point of having braised it and then cover and refrigerate it. Once the eel is braised, you can make the glaze and refrigerate it. When you are ready to make the nigiri, remove the eel from the refrigerator and let it come to room temperature before heating it in the oven. Remove the glaze from the refrigerator at the same time. This is helpful if you are making many different kinds of sushi and you want to get a head start on some of them. This sushi does not require soy sauce for serving.

4 qt/3.8 L water

2 tbsp kosher salt

4 skin-on saltwater eel fillets, about 3 oz/85 g each (see How to Break Down Eel, page 99)

BRAISING LIQUID

2½ cups/600 ml water

½ cup/120 ml sake

5 tbsp/65 g sugar

¼ cup/60 ml soy sauce

4 backbones and 4 heads reserved from preparing 4 eels (optional)

GLAZE

1 tbsp soy sauce

1 tbsp honey

Braising liquid

½ cup/80 g sushi rice (see page 105) at body temperature, covered with a damp kitchen towel

Pinch of sanshō powder

Have ready a large bowl filled with ice water. In a large pot, bring the 4 qt/3.8 L water to a boil over high heat. Add the salt and then the eel fillets to the boiling water. When the skin turns white, after about 3 seconds, remove the fillets and immediately immerse them in the ice water to cool. Remove from the ice water and, using a spoon, gently scrape off the slimy white film on the skin, leaving the skin intact. Rinse the fillets well under cold running water.

To make the braising liquid: In a medium saucepan, combine the 2½ cups/600 ml water, sake, sugar, soy sauce, backbones and heads (if you have them from breaking down the eel).

Add the eel fillets to the braising liquid and bring to a boil over high heat. Lower the heat and simmer, skimming off any impurities that rise to the surface. Place a disk of parchment paper that fits just inside the pan on the surface of the mixture, adjust the heat to a gentle simmer, and cook until tender, 15 to 20 minutes. After 15 minutes, check to see if the eel is tender by gently lifting a fillet out of the braising liquid and pushing softly on the skin side of the fillet. If the skin breaks easily, it is done; if not, return the fillet to the braising liquid, simmer for 5 minutes longer, and test again. Meanwhile, line a sheet pan with aluminum foil.

When the eel fillets are tender, using a long spatula, carefully transfer them to the prepared sheet pan and let them cool. The fillets are very fragile when they are hot, and you don't want to break them. Once the fillets are on the sheet pan, straighten them and spoon some of the braising liquid over them to keep them moist. Strain the rest of the liquid through a fine-mesh sieve and reserve for making the glaze.

To make the glaze: Add the soy sauce and honey to the braising liquid and bring to a boil over high heat. Lower the heat to medium-high and simmer, skimming off any impurities as they rise to the surface, until reduced to a syrupy consistency, about 10 minutes. Remove from the heat, transfer to a heat-proof jar, and let cool to room temperature. (You will not need all of the glaze. The remainder can be stored in an airtight container in the refrigerator for up to 1 month. At sushi bars, this glaze is also paired with octopus, some types of tuna, scallops, mantis shrimp, and such vegetables as shiitake mushrooms and bamboo shoots.) While the glaze is cooling, preheat the oven to 400°F/200°C.

Uncover the sheet pan, place it in the oven, and heat the eel until warm to the touch of the back of your index finger, about 2 minutes.

Following the directions for How to Make Sushi Rice Balls (page 108), make 4 rice balls and place them on a serving plate. Drape a warm eel fillet on each rice ball. Brush a little glaze on each fillet and sprinkle with sanshō powder before serving.

Nigiri with Octopus (Tako)

Octopus is one of Hiro's favorite sushi *neta* (toppings). He loves the taste of octopus, wasabi, and *tsume* (glaze) together. Everything is here—spicy, sweet, sour, umami, and texture. Thinly slice the tentacle on the diagonal and try a piece. (Although they are commonly referred to as tentacles or even legs, they are actually arms). If the octopus is too chewy for you, use the heel of the knife to make small incisions on the surface of each slice using a light hitting motion. This will tenderize the octopus. Some Asian markets carry already-cooked octopus tentacles. Although they will taste a little different from what you cook at home, one can be used here. Choose a tentacle that will yield slices large enough to cover the rice, as pictured on the facing page. This sushi does not require soy sauce for serving.

Following the directions for How to Make Nigiri-zushi (page 124), make 4 nigiri with the rice, octopus, and wasabi. Secure the octopus in place by wrapping a nori strip crosswise around the nigiri at the center of its long side. Make sure the seam of the nori is on the bottom of the nigiri. Place the nigiri on a serving plate, brush the glaze on the octopus, and serve.

½ cup/80 g sushi rice (see page 105) at body temperature, covered with a damp kitchen towel

4 slices cooked octopus tentacle, each 3 by 1 by ³⁄₁₆ in/7.5 cm by 2.5 cm by 5 mm (see How to Break Down and Cook Octopus, page 102)

¼ tsp wasabi

4 strips nori, toasted (see page 112), each 5 by ½ in/12 cm by 12 mm

1 tsp soy glaze (see page 118)

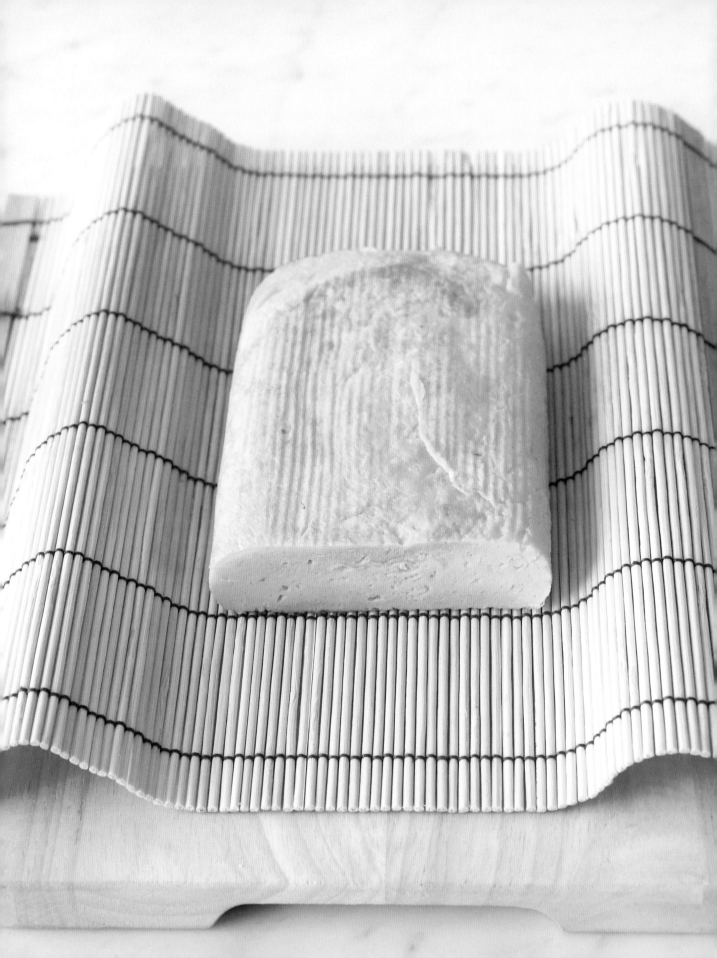

Nigiri with Dashi-flavored Rolled Omelet (Dashi-maki Tamago)

Most people typically eat this nigiri at the end of their sushi meal. It tastes a little bit like dessert because of the slight sweetness of the egg. Sushi chefs also use dashi-maki tamago in the classic *futomaki* (large sushi roll), along with *kampyō* (braised dried gourd strips), cucumber, shiitake mushrooms, and *dembu* (shredded dry-sautéed fish).

½ cup/80 g sushi rice (see page 105) at body temperature, covered with a damp kitchen towel

4 slices Dashi-flavored Rolled Omelet (page 116), each ¾ in/2 cm thick

4 strips nori, toasted (see page 112), each 5½ by ½ in/14 cm by 12 mm

Soy sauce for serving

Following the directions for How to Make Sushi Rice Balls (page 108), make 4 rice balls. Place an omelet slice on each rice ball, and secure the omelet in place by wrapping a nori strip crosswise around the nigiri at the center of its long side. Make sure the seam of the nori is on the bottom of the nigiri. Serve with soy sauce.

Nigiri with Pickled Turnip (Kabu no Tsukemono)

To prepare for this nigiri, pickle the turnip the day before. If the turnip disks are small, you can double up the slices to make one nigiri. You will have more turnip slices and stems than this recipe requires. The pickled turnip is also used in our salmon skin temaki (see page 201), and it makes a great snack. It will keep in a covered container in the refrigerator for 1 week. This sushi does not require soy sauce or wasabi for serving.

1 turnip, about 2½ in/6 cm in diameter

½ tsp kosher salt

Peel from ¼ yuzu or lemon, all white pith removed

½ cup/80 g sushi rice (see page 105) at body temperature, covered with a damp kitchen towel

Cut off the turnip stems and set them aside. Cut the turnip crosswise into disks ¹⁄₁₆ in/2 mm thick. Rinse the stems to remove any dirt and pat dry. Place the turnip and stems in a small bowl, sprinkle with the salt, and gently massage for a couple of minutes. Set aside for 40 minutes, then squeeze the turnip disks and stems in your hands to remove

the excess liquid. Discard any liquid in the bowl and return the turnip disks and stems to the bowl. Cut the yuzu peel into fine julienne, add to the bowl, reserving 4 pieces for garnish, and mix well. Cover with plastic wrap, pressing it directly on the turnip, and place a 1-lb/455-g weight (like a can of vegetables) directly on the turnip to weigh it down. Refrigerate overnight.

Coarsely chop 1 turnip stem and set aside. Pick 4 of the largest turnip disks to make the nigiri.

Following the directions for How to Make Nigiri-zushi (page 124), make 4 nigiri with the rice, replacing the fish with the turnip (and omitting the wasabi). Place the nigiri on a serving plate. Top each nigiri with ¼ tsp of the chopped stem, mounding it in the center of the turnip disk. Garnish each stem mound with a piece of the reserved yuzu, then serve.

Nigiri with Braised Daikon

When daikon is braised, it stays firm but takes on a beautiful, luscious texture. The seasoned liquid in which it is cooked helps mask some of its strong odor and round out its flavor. Because this nigiri has a light flavor, we like to eat it at the beginning of the meal. This sushi does not require soy sauce or wasabi for serving.

1 cup/240 ml dashi (see page 114)

1 tbsp mirin

2 tsp light soy sauce

4 pieces peeled daikon, each 4 by 1¼ by ¼ in/10 cm by 3 cm by 6 mm

½ cup/80 g sushi rice (see page 105) at body temperature, covered with a damp kitchen towel

4 strips nori, toasted (see page 112), each 6 by ½ in/15 cm by 12 mm

1 tsp peeled and grated ginger

¼ tsp shichimi togarashi or dried chile flakes

¼ tsp grated or finely chopped lime zest

In a small saucepan, combine the dashi, mirin, soy sauce, and daikon pieces; place over medium-high heat; and bring to a boil. Lower the heat to a simmer and skim off any impurities that rise to the surface. Place a disk of parchment paper that fits just inside the pan on the surface of the mixture, adjust the heat to a gentle simmer, cover with a lid, and simmer gently until the tip of a small knife goes through the daikon but the daikon is not mushy, about 5 minutes. Remove from the heat and let the daikon cool in the cooking liquid. Transfer to a small container, cover, and refrigerate until using. Just before using, pat the daikon dry.

Following the directions for How to Make Sushi Rice Balls (page 108), make 4 rice balls. Place a piece of the braised daikon on the top of each ball, and secure the daikon in place by wrapping a nori strip crosswise around the nigiri at the center of its long side. Make sure the seam of the nori is on the bottom of the nigiri. Place the nigiri on a serving plate. Put a small amount of the ginger in the center of each piece of daikon. Sprinkle the shichimi togarashi and lime zest evenly over the nigiri and serve.

Nigiri with Grilled Shiitake Mushrooms

Mushrooms are a versatile ingredient. Growers have learned how to cultivate many varieties, which gives great freedom in creating nigiri with mushrooms. Most mushrooms have such a strong umami quality that they give the impression of eating meat. That may be one of the reasons we like them so much. If you try grilling thinner mushrooms, such as *maitake*, *matsutake*, abalone, chanterelle, or button, the same way we grill shiitake mushrooms here, spray a little sake or water onto them when they are cooking to prevent them from drying out. This sushi is pictured at bottom on the facing page.

4 shiitake mushrooms, with caps about 3 in/7.5 cm in diameter, stems removed

Kosher salt

½ cup/80 g sushi rice (see page 105) at body temperature, covered with a damp kitchen towel

1 tsp spicy grated daikon (see page 121)

¼ tsp finely chopped fresh chives

Soy sauce for serving

Heat a charcoal or gas grill or a stove-top grill pan to medium-high; you should be able to hold your palm 4 in/10 cm above the heat for no more than 5 seconds.

Place the mushroom caps, top-side down, on the grill rack or pan and cook for about 2 minutes. Flip the caps over and grill until well cooked and soft to the touch, about 2 minutes longer. Sprinkle with a little salt, remove from the grill or pan, and let the caps cool just until they can be handled.

Following the directions for How to Make Nigiri-zushi (page 124), make 4 nigiri with the rice and replace the fish with the mushrooms, cap-side up (but do not add any wasabi). This will make a finished nigiri with the mushroom gill-side up. Place the nigiri on a serving plate. Divide the grated daikon evenly among the nigiri, mounding it on the center of the mushroom, and sprinkle the chives evenly over the daikon. Serve with soy sauce.

Nigiri with Grilled King Trumpet Mushrooms (Eringi) and Mountain Caviar (Tonburi)

Known as *eringi* in Japanese, the king trumpet mushroom, with its thick, white, fleshy stem and small, thin cap, is a type of oyster mushroom now widely available in American markets. *Tonburi* are the seeds of *Bassia scoparia*, a bushy shrub native to Europe and Asia known as *houkigi* in Japanese. They resemble caviar, both in appearance and texture, and are sometimes called mountain or land caviar. Their taste is more reminiscent of nuts than of the costly fish roe, however. Look for tonburi in the refrigerated section of Japanese or other Asian markets. This sushi, pictured at the top of the photograph on page 161, does not require soy sauce for serving.

2 king trumpet mushrooms, about 1¼ in/3 cm in diameter and 3 in/7.5 cm long with stems intact

½ tsp ponzu sauce (page 119)

½ cup/80 g sushi rice (see page 105) at body temperature, covered with a damp kitchen towel

¼ tsp wasabi

2 tsp tonburi

Heat a charcoal or gas grill or a stove-top grill pan to medium-high; you should be able to hold your palm 4 in/10 cm above the heat for no more than 5 seconds. While the grill is heating, cut the mushrooms in half lengthwise. Score the cut side of each mushroom on the diagonal in a ¼-in/6-mm diamond pattern.

Put the mushroom halves, cut-side down, on the grill rack or pan and cook until light golden brown, about 3 minutes. Flip the halves over and cook until soft to the touch, about 1 minute longer. Transfer them, cut-side up, to a plate and let cool to body temperature, then sprinkle with the ponzu sauce.

Following the directions for How to Make Nigiri-zushi (page 124), make 4 nigiri, using the rice and wasabi and replacing the fish with the mushroom, cut-side up. Place the nigiri on a serving plate. Divide the tonburi evenly among the nigiri, mounding it on the center of the mushroom, then serve.

Nigiri with Grilled Eggplant (Yaki Nasu)

This nigiri, pictured at the top of the photograph on page 164, is one of our favorite sushi in summertime. Pick eggplants that have dark-purple tender skin, a firm body, and no brown spots. We prefer to use Japanese eggplants that are slender and of medium length. Because they are younger at this size, they also have smaller seeds. You can use other varieties, but look for slender eggplants rather than the globe type. If you cannot find eggplants 4 in/10 cm long, look for an eggplant about double the length and cut it in half crosswise.

2 Japanese eggplants, about 4 in/10 cm long and 1½ in/4 cm in diameter at broadest part

½ cup/80 g sushi rice (see page 105) at body temperature, covered with a damp kitchen towel

⅛ tsp peeled and grated ginger

1 tsp finely shredded dried bonito flakes (optional)

⅛ tsp finely chopped fresh chives

Soy sauce for serving

Heat a charcoal or gas grill or a stove-top grill pan to medium-high; you should be able to hold your palm 4 in/10 cm above the heat for no more than 5 seconds. Place the whole eggplants on the grill rack or pan and cook, turning as needed, until the entire surface is soft and the eggplants are cooked through, 6 to 8 minutes. Remove the eggplants from the rack or pan and let cool until they can be handled, then cut off the stems, carefully peel off the skin, and cut in half lengthwise.

Following the directions for How to Make Sushi Rice Balls (page 108), make 4 rice balls and place them on a serving plate. Drape the eggplant pieces, cut-side down, over the rice balls. Put an equal amount of the grated ginger on the center of each eggplant piece, and mound the bonito flakes (if using) on the ginger. Sprinkle the chives over the top and serve with soy sauce.

Nigiri with Dashi-marinated Roasted Bell Pepper (Piiman)

This may sound a little strange for sushi, but when made well it looks like tuna (see facing page, bottom) and tastes terrific. Although we would suggest that you roast your own peppers, if you are pressed for time, good store-bought roasted peppers are available and can be substituted. Just be sure to purchase them in their own liquid or in water, not in oil or in a vinegar solution. This sushi does not require soy sauce or wasabi for serving.

¼ cup/60 ml dashi (see page 114)

Kosher salt

1 red bell pepper

4 jalapeño chile slices, each ⅛ in/3 mm thick, seeded

½ cup/80 g sushi rice (see page 105) at body temperature, covered with a damp kitchen towel

1 tsp soy glaze (see page 118; optional)

Put the dashi in a small container with a flat bottom measuring about 4 by 2 in/10 by 5 cm, and season with a little salt. Set aside.

Using tongs, hold the bell pepper over the burner of a gas stove turned on to medium-high (or place a small metal grid over the burner and place the pepper on it). Turn the pepper as needed until the skin is charred black and blistered on all sides. (If you do not have a gas stove, grill the pepper on an outdoor grill over a medium-hot fire or under a preheated broiler close to the heat source. If broiling the pepper, check it often to make sure the skin is charring but the pepper is not overcooking. The broiler is a hotter environment, and the pepper flesh must remain firm.) Transfer the pepper to a small container with a lid, or to a small bowl and cover with plastic wrap. Let stand for 15 minutes. This ensures that the heat of the pepper will cook the flesh at the same time that the smokiness from the charring permeates it. (If using a broiler, check after 5 minutes; the char should come off easily and the flesh should still be slightly firm to the touch.)

Remove the pepper from the container. Cut off the stem end of the pepper, then slit open one side of the pepper lengthwise and remove the seeds. Peel off the blistered skin completely. If necessary, use a paper towel to remove small particles of the charred skin. Cut the cleaned pepper into four rectangles, each 3 by 1 in/7.5 by 2.5 cm. Put the pepper rectangles into the seasoned dashi and marinate for at least 3 hours, or up to overnight.

When the bell pepper is ready to use, lightly char the jalapeño slices on a small metal grid or a stove-top grill pan placed over medium-high heat or with a butane kitchen torch. Remove the pepper rectangles from the dashi and place them on a paper towel to remove the excess moisture.

Following the directions for How to Make Sushi Rice Balls (page 108), make 4 rice balls. Top each ball with a pepper piece, taking the time to mold the pepper over the rice so that it is smooth and resembles tuna. Place the nigiri on a serving plate. Put a jalapeño slice on the center of each pepper piece, brush the pepper and jalapeño with the glaze (if using), and serve.

How to

Make Gunkan-maki (Warship Rolls)

Gunkan-maki, which were invented in Tokyo in the early 1940s, are a relative newcomer to the sushi menu. *Gunkan* means "warship," and the oval-shaped rice balls wrapped with strips of nori and served on a *geta*, the classic wooden sushi serving tray, are thought to look like a fleet of warships. This is a great way to make individual sushi you want to top with a diced ingredient, like chopped tuna, or a slippery ingredient, like salmon roe, that won't stay on top of a traditional nigiri.

FOR 4 GUNKAN-MAKI

½ cup/80 g sushi rice (see page 105) at body temperature, covered with a damp kitchen towel

1 sheet nori, toasted (see page 112), cut into 4 strips each 6 by 1 in/15 by 2.5 cm

Wasabi, as specified in individual recipes

Topping(s), as specified in individual recipes

Following the directions for How to Make Sushi Rice Balls (page 108), make 4 rice balls (1). With the rough side of the nori facing inward, wrap a nori strip around the perimeter of the rice ball, starting at the middle of a long side (2). Continue wrapping until it overlaps the other end of the nori (3,4). Wrap the next rice ball and place it right next to the first one, with the overlapped side against the overlapped side of the first roll. This will hold the end of the nori strip attached to the roll. Repeat the process for the remaining two rolls, always keeping the overlapped side against the side of the previous ball (5). Top as directed in individual recipes (6) before serving.

Note: Do not make gunkan-maki too far in advance. The moisture in the rice will wilt the nori and make it tough. If you are assembling a selection of sushi, make the gunkan-maki last.

1

2

3

4

5

6

Gunkan-maki with Broiled Sake-marinated Black Cod (Gindara)

Fresh black cod, which is available year-round, is very special to us. Sake-marinated black cod has been the signature dish at Terra since the opening. The flaky rich meat has a unique taste and texture. Black cod has the added bonus of being a difficult fish to overcook. Its natural gelatin keeps it moist even if it is cooked for a couple of minutes too long.

Kinome, the young leaves from the Japanese pepper (prickly ash) tree, have a unique floral aroma with a bit of spice. Unfortunately, they are both seasonal (early spring) and hard to find in the United States, unless you know someone who has a tree, or occasionally a Japanese fish supplier will part with some sprigs. Kaffir lime leaves can be substituted; remove the thick vein from the center of each leaf and finely julienne the leaves before using. This sushi does not require soy sauce or wasabi for serving.

SAKE MARINADE

1¼ tsp sake

1¼ tsp mirin

2½ tsp soy sauce

1¾ tsp sugar

Pinch of peeled and grated fresh ginger

Pinch of grated garlic

5 oz/140 g black cod fillet without skin, about 3 by 3 by 1 in/7.5 by 7.5 by 2.5 cm thick

4 pieces gunkan-maki (see page 166)

Leaves from 2 sprigs kinome (optional)

Pinch of freshly ground white pepper

To make the marinade: In a small bowl, whisk together the sake, mirin, soy sauce, sugar, ginger, and garlic. Set aside 1 tsp of the marinade to use as a glaze.

Place the cod fillet in a small resealable bag and add the marinade. Remove as much of the air as possible from the bag, seal it closed, and refrigerate for at least 3 hours, or up to 24 hours, turning the bag every 30 minutes to marinate the fish evenly.

Preheat the broiler to high. Using a paper towel, pat the cod dry, then place it in a small broiler-proof pan, put the pan under the broiler, and broil until the fish turns deep brown, about 5 minutes. Turn the heat to medium (or move the pan farther from the heat source) and continue to cook until the cod is cooked through, about 5 minutes. One

way to check for doneness is to look for small bones poking through the top surface of the fillet. If they are visible and they come out easily when tugged with tweezers, the fish is ready. The best way to check is to insert the tip of a thin-bladed knife into the fillet, pull it out, and check the temperature carefully against your lip. If the knife tip is very hot, the cod is cooked through. Remove from the broiler and let cool slightly until the fillet can be easily handled.

Gently separate the cooked fish into flakes (if the fish is properly cooked, the flakes will be easy to separate). Divide the cod flakes among the gunkan-maki. Drizzle the reserved glaze evenly over the cod. Arrange about 5 kinome leaves (if using) on the cod on each sushi, sprinkle with the white pepper, and serve.

Gunkan-maki with Horse Mackerel (Aji) and Japanese Ginger (Myōga)

In sushi bars, you will encounter three distinct types of mackerel: Atlantic (*saba*), Spanish (*sawara*), and horse (*aji*). Of this trio, horse mackerel, which is lighter and cleaner tasting that the others, is the most common and is the one that should be used for this sushi.

The spicy, floral flavor of *myōga*, commonly known in English as Japanese ginger, is milder than ginger. Traditionally a seasonal plant, the appearance of crisp, newly sprouted myōga is a welcome sign that the summer season is starting. The Japanese have a saying that if you eat too much myōga, it will make you forgetful or stupid—a fitting homage to an ingredient that is so prized! If you cannot find it in your local markets, you can replace it with equal parts thinly sliced shallot and ginger. This sushi does not require soy sauce or wasabi for serving.

¼ cup/45 g diced (¼ in/6 mm) skinned horse mackerel fillet (see How to Break Down Small Fish, page 69)

1 tsp thinly sliced Japanese ginger

1 tsp flying fish roe

Pinch of grated lime zest

½ tsp light soy sauce

4 pieces gunkan-maki (see page 166)

In a small bowl, combine the mackerel, Japanese ginger, roe, lime zest, and soy sauce and stir to mix well. Spoon the mixture onto the gunkan-maki, dividing it evenly, and serve.

Gunkan-maki with Lightly Poached West Coast Oysters (Kaki)

You might expect that oyster sushi would feature raw oysters but we prefer to poach the oysters, which gives them a slight firmness that we like. When you eat this gunkan-maki, the ocean flavor from the oyster bursts through. We suggest that you try one with soy sauce and one without to see which way you prefer, but do not use wasabi. This sushi is pictured at top on the facing page.

YUZU MISO

8 cups/2 L water

1 yuzu or ½ lemon

¼ cup/65 g white miso

2 tsp mirin

2 tsp sake

1 tbsp sugar

1 cup/240 ml dashi (see page 114)

2 tbsp mirin

2 tbsp soy sauce

Pinch of peeled and grated fresh ginger

4 freshly shucked small oysters (about the size of your thumb)

4 pieces gunkan-maki (see page 166)

4 very fine strips yuzu or lemon zest

Soy sauce for serving (optional)

To make the yuzu miso: In a medium-size saucepan, bring the water to a boil over high heat. Meanwhile, with a vegetable peeler, remove the zest from the yuzu, being careful not to remove any of the white pith. Set the remainder of the fruit aside. Finely mince the citrus zest. When the water is boiling, drop in the zest and blanch for 3 seconds to remove the bitterness. Drain into a fine-mesh sieve, rinse under cold running water, drain again, and pat dry with a paper towel.

Have ready a large bowl filled with ice water. Juice the peeled yuzu. In a small saucepan, combine the yuzu zest and juice, miso, mirin, sake, and sugar and bring to a boil over medium heat, stirring constantly with a wooden spatula. Lower the heat to a gentle simmer and cook, continuing to stir, until the mixture is the consistency of ketchup, about 3 minutes. Remove from the heat and put the pan in the ice water to cool. You will have more sauce than you need for this recipe. Remove 2 tbsp of the sauce and reserve. Transfer the remaining sauce to a small nonreactive container, cover, and refrigerate for up to

1 week. (Bring the sauce to room temperature before using. It will complement mackerel, octopus, and mushrooms and other vegetables.)

Refresh the ice water bath used for cooling the sauce. In a small saucepan, combine the dashi, mirin, soy sauce, and ginger; place over high heat; and heat to 145°F/63°C. Place the oysters in the cooking liquid and bring the temperature back to 145°F/63°C, then immediately remove the pan from the heat. Place the pan in the ice water and cool the oysters to body temperature, then remove the oysters from the cooking liquid and pat dry.

Place an oyster on each gunkan-maki, spoon 1½ tsp of the yuzu miso onto the center of each oyster, and place a strip of yuzu zest on the yuzu miso. Serve immediately, with soy sauce, if desired, while the oysters are still warm.

Gunkan-maki with Butter-sautéed Monterey Abalone (Awabi)

Warm, buttery, tender abalone and vinegary sushi rice are one of the best culinary matches. Presenting abalone in a gunkan-maki is a natural pairing because abalones eat seaweed. Abalone is successfully farmed in many coastal areas; in California alone, some half-dozen farms exist, plus a farm in Hawaii uses deep water and its own home-grown seaweed. These farms, which produce some of the finest and freshest abalones, maintain the great tradition of producing food from the sea through sustainable aquaculture. This sushi, pictured at the bottom of the photograph on page 171, does not require soy sauce or wasabi for serving.

1 live abalone in the shell, about 2¾ oz/75 g or 2½ in/6 cm long and 2 in/5 cm wide

½ cup/120 ml dashi (see page 114)

Fine sea salt

1 tsp sake

4 pieces gunkan-maki (see page 166)

4½ tsp unsalted butter

Dash of fresh Meyer lemon juice

¼ tsp finely chopped fresh chives

Coarse sea salt

Clean the abalone under cold running water. Run a pallet knife (flat, flexible, blunt blade) along the entire edge of the abalone, slowly increasing the pressure until the knife is at the bottom of the shell. Once the circumference of the shell has been released, the abalone will come out easily. An abalone looks like an upside-down anvil, the part that you see on the underside of the shell is the foot and is smaller than the larger muscle in the shell. Remove the internal organs, which are around the outside of the foot and should come off easily with your fingers. Discard them all except for the liver, which is crescent-shaped, about ¾ in/2 cm in diameter, and ranges from a beige green to a dark green. Place the liver in a small saucepan, add the dashi, and cook over low heat for 2 minutes. Remove the pan from the heat and let the liver cool in the liquid.

Transfer the liver to a cutting board and reserve the cooking liquid. Finely chop the liver, then push the side of the knife against the liver to form a stiff paste. Transfer the paste to a small bowl, add a little of the cooking liquid, and whisk to make a thick paste. Season with fine sea salt and set aside.

Place the abalone, larger flat-side down and foot-side up, on a cutting board and cut it cross-wise into slices ⅛ in/3 mm thick. You should end up with 20 to 24 slices. Transfer them to a small bowl, sprinkle with the sake, and toss well.

Place the gunkan-maki on the cutting board. With your index finger, smear an equal amount of the liver paste on the middle of each rice ball.

In a small sauté pan, melt the butter over high heat. When the butter begins to turn light brown and smells a little nutty, add the abalone slices and sauté quickly until warmed through, about 3 seconds. Remove from the heat, add the lemon juice, and toss quickly. Transfer the abalone slices to a paper towel to blot any extra fat.

Divide the slices evenly among the gunkan-maki. Sprinkle evenly with the chives, top with a little coarse sea salt, and serve immediately while warm.

Gunkan-maki with West Coast Sea Urchin (Uni)

Uni (sea urchin) is one of our favorite sushi ingredients. Lissa especially adores this sea creature. A long time ago, when we were in Kyoto, we were having a dinner in a family-run *kappo* restaurant (a fine-dining counter-style establishment where diners watch the chef prepare their food). We saw an older man eating a whole box of sea urchin by himself! Lissa was so excited that she asked Hiro to ask the chef whether she could have a box also. Luckily, she got what she requested and finished the whole box. (She did give Hiro a couple of bites.) West Coast sea urchins are bigger and milder flavored than sea urchins harvested on the East Coast. Each tongue (the term used for the striplike pieces of roe) is about the size of your little finger. East Coast tongues are not only smaller and slightly stronger flavored but are also darker.

Place the gunkan-maki on a cutting board. Use your index finger to smear an equal amount of the wasabi on the middle of each rice ball. Spoon the sea urchin evenly onto the gunkan-maki and serve with soy sauce, lemon juice, and salt.

One pair of gunkan-maki is the typical order at a sushi bar. We like to eat one dipped in soy sauce and the other one sprinkled with a little lemon juice and sea salt.

4 pieces gunkan-maki (see page 166)

¼ tsp wasabi

12 tongues sea urchin roe, about 3½ oz/100 g

Soy sauce and/or fresh lemon juice and sea salt for serving

Gunkan-maki with Salmon Roe (Ikura)

This sushi is fun to eat whether you use salmon roe or another kind of roe, because the eggs like to pop and jump around in your mouth. At sushi bars, you will see people using their chopsticks to steal a couple of the eggs from the top of a gunkan-maki to eat by themselves. They are childlike fun, which makes them hard to resist. This is also one of the simplest and most beautiful sushi to make. No matter what type of roe you use, make sure it is the freshest available and is refrigerated when you purchase it. Pasteurized roe that does not need refrigeration is available in some stores. We do not recommend it, however, as the eggs are soft and very salty. This sushi does not require soy sauce or wasabi.

Place the gunkan-maki on a cutting board. Use your index finger to smear an equal amount of the wasabi on the middle of each rice ball. Spoon 1 tbsp of the roe onto each rice ball. Sprinkle the lemon zest evenly over the roe.

If using the quail egg yolks, make a small indentation in the center of each spoonful of roe and gently place the yolk in the indentation and serve.

Variation: Replace the salmon roe with another type of fish roe, such as ocean trout roe, American sturgeon caviar, flying fish roe, or capelin roe. Or, mix roes of different colors.

**4 pieces gunkan-maki
(see page 166)**

¼ tsp wasabi

4 tbsp/75 g salmon roe

⅛ tsp grated or very finely chopped lemon zest

**4 quail egg yolks
(see page 34; optional)**

Gunkan-maki with Grilled Cod Milt (Shirako)

In winter, we get fresh cod milt from the Boston area, which is a treat for sushi lovers. Cod milt has a wonderfully smooth texture, almost like silken tofu. You can eat it raw or poached, but we find that grilling it adds more depth of flavor. The toasty aroma and warmth against the sushi rice is a memorable combination. This sushi does not require soy sauce or wasabi for serving.

Now the question is, can you tell your guests with a straight face that cod milt is cod sperm?

One 4-oz/115-g piece fresh cod milt

2 cups/480 ml water

½ tsp rice vinegar

½ tsp kosher salt

4 pieces gunkan-maki (see page 166)

1 tsp spicy grated daikon (see page 121)

½ tsp finely chopped fresh chives

¾ tsp ponzu sauce (page 119)

Soak the cod milt in ice water to cover for 1 hour. Drain and pat dry with a paper towel.

Heat a charcoal or gas grill or a stove-top grill pan to medium. If using a grill, place a grill screen over the grill rack. The cod milt is very soft and needs to be supported.

While the grill or grill pan is heating, in a small saucepan, combine the water, vinegar, and salt and bring to a boil. Add the cod milt and cook gently until the outside tightens a little bit, about 1 minute. Be careful that you do not overcook the milt, as you want it to stay creamy. Drain and pat dry with a paper towel.

Cut the cod milt into 4 equal slices. Place the slices on the grill screen or pan and grill, turning once, until golden brown, about 1 minute on each side.

Place a slice of the cod milt on each gunkan-maki. Put a small ball of the grated daikon on the center of each slice and sprinkle evenly with the chives. Spoon the ponzu over the daikon, dividing it evenly, and serve.

Gunkan-maki with Three Slimes: Okra, Mountain Yam, and Natto

Despite the strange name, this is one of our favorite versions of sushi. We call it "three slimes" because there are three different types of slimy ingredients in the mix. It is a great combination texturally, as it marries crunch and softness. The Japanese regard this blend as an aphrodisiac.

Each of the three ingredients used for this gunkan-maki is distinctive but all share the common trait of sliminess. Most Americans know okra, the pods of which release a viscous liquid when cut. Available in Japanese markets, *yama-imo* or *naga-imo*, known in English as the Japanese mountain yam, is a little longer than a daikon root and has hairy, light brown skin and white flesh. Like okra, it releases a slimy liquid when cut. *Natto* (fermented soybeans) has a flavor people often compare to that of a stinky cheese and is sticky and slippery at the same time. This sushi does not require soy sauce or wasabi for serving.

1 tbsp diced (¼ in/6 mm) blanched okra (from about 2 medium-size pods, each about 2 in/5 cm long)

1 tbsp diced (¼ in/6 mm) peeled mountain yam

2 tbsp natto

1 quail egg (see page 34; optional)

1 tsp light soy sauce

½ tsp finely chopped green onion, white part only or white and tender green part

½ tsp wasabi

4 pieces gunkan-maki (see page 166)

In a medium-size bowl, combine the okra, mountain yam, natto, egg (if using), soy sauce, green onion, and wasabi and mix vigorously to aerate. Spoon the mixture evenly onto the gunkan-maki and serve.

Variation: This mixture also works well in a temaki (see page 198) or hosomaki (see page 182).

Gunkan-maki with Avocado and Charred Jalapeño

If you think of the flavors of guaca-mole, you will get a feeling for this sushi. It is surprising how the tex-ture of the rice combined with the creamy richness of the avocado makes the avocado seem even richer. The addition of the charred jalapeño wakes you up the moment you smell it. Because the chile is under the avocado, it is a surprise burst of flavor and heat, so be prepared!

1 small jalapeño chile, about 2 in/5 cm long

½ Hass avocado, peeled

4 pieces gunkan-maki (see page 166)

½ slice lime, ¹⁄₁₆ in/2 mm thick

Soy sauce for serving

Heat a charcoal or gas grill or a stove-top grill pan to medium-high; you should be able to hold your palm 4 in/10 cm above the heat for no more than 5 seconds.

Place the chile on the grill rack or pan and grill, turning as needed, until charred and blistered on all sides. Remove from the grill, and when cool enough to handle, remove the charred skin with a small knife. Any areas where the skin is not charred, the skin will not come off easily, and it is fine to leave it on. Cut the stem off of the chile, quarter the chile length-wise, and remove and discard the seeds. If you prefer less heat, cut away the white membrane that held the seeds, as well.

Cut the avocado half in half lengthwise, then cut crosswise into slices ¼ in/6 mm thick.

Place a jalapeño quarter on the top of the rice in each gunkan-maki. Divide the avocado slices evenly among the gunkan-maki, arranging them attractively on the jalapeño. Cut the lime slice into quarters, and place a lime wedge on the center of the avocado slices on each sushi. Serve with soy sauce.

Sushi Rolls
(Maki-zushi)

Make Hosomaki (Skinny Rolls)

In the United States, sheets of nori are now sold not only in Asian markets but also in many supermarkets. Make sure that you buy Japanese nori sheets that measure about 8 by 7½ in/ 20 by 19 cm (see page 26 for more information on nori). Each sheet can be used to make two hosomaki: place the sheet on a cutting board with a long side facing you and cut in half horizontally. If you find a range of prices, spend a little more money on a good-quality nori, as it will improve the taste of your sushi rolls.

Be sure you use a bamboo sushi mat with thin bamboo strips for rolling these skinny rolls (see page 35 for more information on sushi mats). Nori has a rough side and a smoother, shiny side. When rolling, you want the rough side facing up so that the shiny side is visible when the roll is completed, making for a nicer presentation. The main ingredient or ingredients for filling each roll should measure about ¼ cup/60 ml. If the filling is chopped fish, it should weigh 2½ oz/70 g. If the filling is in stick form, such as cucumber, daikon, or even fish, it should fit in an area of ⅜ by ⅜ by 7½ in/ 1 by 1 by 19 cm.

½ sheet nori, toasted (see page 112)

Hand water (see page 113)

½ cup/80 g sushi rice (see page 105) at body temperature, covered with a damp kitchen towel

Wasabi, as specified in individual recipes

Ingredient(s) for filling roll, as specified in individual recipes

Place a bamboo sushi mat, shiny-side up, on your work surface, with the bamboo sticks running horizontally. The mat should be completely dry so that the nori remains dry and crisp. Place the nori sheet, rough-side up and a long side facing you, on the mat.

Moisten the palm of one hand lightly with the hand water, then rub your hands together to moisten them. Pick up the rice (1) and place it on the center of the nori sheet. Moisten your hands again, and using just your finger-tips, spread the rice, using a gentle pinching motion (2). It is important not to smash or com-press the rice, as you want it to stay fluffy. Create an even layer of rice covering almost the entire nori sheet, leaving ½ in/12 mm uncovered along the long edge farthest from you (3). Remoisten your hands as necessary to keep the rice from sticking to your fingers, but be careful not to use too much water or the rice will lose its stickiness. Using your fingertips, pinch the rice to create a low, narrow ridge of rice along the front edge nearest you. This will keep the filling in place.

If the recipe calls for wasabi, use your index finger to scoop the wasabi and smear it horizontally across the rice just inside the ridge, extending it from one side to the other. Evenly place the main ingredient or ingredients on top of the wasabi (4).

To start rolling, put one hand on each side of the nori sheet and, with your thumbs under the near corners of the mat, start to roll (5), lifting up the edge of the mat and immediately moving your hands along the front edge to flip the nori up and over the filling away from you (6). Complete the roll by meeting the front edge of the roll to the rice (7). Hold the nori in place while pulling back gently on the rolled portion of the mat to tighten. Continue rolling, always keeping the roll snug so the filling stays in place, until you reach the far end of the nori. Hold the mat to tighten again, pulling slightly toward you to seal (8).

Position the finished roll horizon-tally on a dry cutting board. Place the tip of your slicing knife into the hand water, then lift the tip up vertically to moisten the length of the blade. With the moistened blade, cut the roll in half cross-wise (9). Place the halves hori-zontally side by side, hold them together with one hand, and slice them crosswise into thirds to create six equal-size pieces (10,11). If the knife becomes sticky between cuts, wipe the blade with a moist towel to remove the rice and moisten the blade again before the next cut.

Arrange the rolls on a plate, with some pieces standing on their sides and others lying down, and serve.

How to
Make Hosomaki (Skinny Rolls)

1

2   >>>

5

6

3

4

7

8

How to

Make Hosomaki (Skinny Rolls)

9

10

11

Hosomaki with Tuna (Maguro)

Some types of sushi are considered the basics, and a tuna roll is one of them—a sushi style that almost everyone encounters on his or her first trip to a sushi bar. This roll is so simple—just two ingredients, tuna and green onions—that most of us don't even bother to order it when we are at a sushi bar. But if you do decide to try one, either at a sushi bar or at home, it will produce a sweet memory of the first time you ate a maguro maki.

¼ cup/70 g chopped tuna loin

½ tsp chopped green onion, white part only or white and tender green part

½ sheet nori, toasted (see page 112)

½ cup/80 g sushi rice (see page 105) at body temperature, covered with a damp kitchen towel

¼ tsp wasabi

Soy sauce for serving

In a small bowl, toss together the tuna and green onion.

Following the directions for How to Make Hosomaki (page 182), make 1 roll with the nori, rice, wasabi, and tuna-onion mixture. Slice the roll and serve with soy sauce.

Hosomaki with Squid (Ika) and Natto

Ika natto, a mixture of squid and fermented soybeans, respectively, is one of Lissa's favorite combinations, and the reason they go together so well is because their textures—slippery—are so complementary. Lissa was first introduced to natto in Hiro's hometown of Ichihasama, in Miyagi Prefecture on Honshu. His mother serves it mixed with a variety of ingredients, such as raw shrimp, squid, garlic, chives, and egg yolk, as part of breakfast every morning. We even visited a local natto factory, but we weren't allowed to go inside. It seems that the owner thought we might steal his secret recipe.

1 tbsp diced squid, in ¼-in/6-mm squares (see How to Break Down Squid, page 100)

1 tbsp natto

½ tsp chopped green onion, white part only or white and tender green part

⅛ tsp Japanese mustard

½ sheet nori, toasted (see page 112)

½ cup/80 g sushi rice (see page 105) at body temperature, covered with a damp kitchen towel

¼ tsp wasabi

Soy sauce for serving

In a small bowl, combine the squid, natto, green onion, and mustard and mix vigorously to aerate.

Following the directions for How to Make Hosomaki (page 182), make 1 roll with the nori, rice, wasabi, and squid mixture. Slice the roll and serve with soy sauce.

Hosomaki with Herring Roe (Kazunoko)

In winter, *kazunoko* (herring roe) is one of Japan's seasonal delicacies and an important part of a family's New Year's Day meal, symbolizing both prosperity and fertility. The crunchy texture of the roe is unique, and don't be surprised if someone next to you gives you a funny look when they hear the crunch of the eggs as you eat them. If you are pressed for time, you can purchase the roe already marinated in Japanese markets. This sushi does not require soy sauce for serving.

3 oz/85 g herring roe

1 tbsp kosher salt

⅓ cup/80 ml dashi (see page 114)

1½ tsp light soy sauce

1½ tsp mirin

1½ tsp sake

⅛ tsp sugar

1 tbsp small dried bonito flakes

Pinch of dried chile flakes

½ sheet nori, toasted (see page 112)

½ cup/80 g sushi rice (see page 105) at body temperature, covered with a damp kitchen towel

¼ tsp wasabi

Rinse the herring roe in cold running water, place in a nonreactive container, sprinkle with the salt, and toss well. Cover with plastic and refrigerate overnight.

The next day, pour 3 qt/2.8 L water into a medium-size bowl, add the herring roe, cover, and let soak in the refrigerator for 4 hours. Drain, pat dry with a paper towel, and then gently peel the membrane off of the egg sac. Refill the bowl with 3 qt/2.8 L water, add the herring roe, and let soak in the refrigerator for 8 hours, changing the water at least three times during the process. Remove the roe from the water and pat dry with a paper towel.

While the roe is soaking, make a marinade. Have ready a medium-size bowl filled with ice water. In a small saucepan, combine the dashi, soy sauce, mirin, sake, sugar, bonito flakes, and dried chile flakes and bring to a boil over high heat. Remove from the heat, strain through a fine-mesh sieve into a heat-proof bowl, and place the bowl in the ice water.

Once the liquid is completely chilled, add the herring roe and let marinate overnight. When ready to make the herring roll, remove the roe from the marinade and pat dry. The roe should weigh about 2½ oz/70 g. Split the roe in half lengthwise.

Following the directions for How to Make Hosomaki (page 182), make 1 roll with the nori, rice, wasabi, and herring roe. If the roe is irregularly shaped, trim it to as even a thickness as possible before arranging it on the wasabi. Add the trimmings to any places where the roe is thinner. Slice the roll and serve.

Note: The marinated herring roe will keep for 1 week in the refrigerator.

Hosomaki with Cucumber (Kyūri)

The *kappa* is one of the water spirits of Japan, a mythical animal that lives in ponds and rivers. It is child-size, looks like a combination of a turtle and a frog, and has a beak like a bird. The kappa is a mischievous spirit and is humorously said to like cucumbers to eat more than children. For that reason, cucumber rolls are called *kappa maki* and are a favorite of children in Japan.

Following the directions for How to Make Hosomaki (page 182), make 1 roll with the nori, rice, wasabi, and cucumber. Slice the roll and serve with soy sauce.

½ sheet nori, toasted (see page 112)

½ cup/80 g sushi rice (see page 105) at body temperature, covered with a damp kitchen towel

¼ tsp wasabi

1 piece Japanese cucumber, about ⅜ in/1 cm square and 8 in/20 cm long

Soy sauce for serving

Hosomaki with Pickled Plum (Uméboshi), Cucumber (Kyūri), and Shiso

We often eat this roll at the end of the meal, where it serves as a palate cleanser. The sourness of the uméboshi has a cleansing effect, the shiso imparts brightness, and the cucumber contributes crunch. We like to buy whole uméboshi, which typically come with some red shiso pickled along with the plums. You can use that in the roll as a substitute for the fresh shiso if you have problems finding the latter. If you want to opt for ease, look for umé paste in a tube. This sushi does not require soy sauce or wasabi for serving.

Following the directions for How to Make Hosomaki (page 182), place the nori on the mat, cover with the rice, and sprinkle the rice with the sesame seeds. Using your finger, smear the uméboshi across the rice in place of the wasabi. Arrange the shiso and cucumber on the uméboshi, then roll up and slice as directed to serve.

½ sheet nori, toasted (see page 112)

½ cup/80 g sushi rice (see page 105) at body temperature, covered with a damp kitchen towel

Pinch of sesame seeds, toasted (see page 34)

½ tsp chopped uméboshi

½ shiso leaf, cut in chiffonade

1 piece Japanese cucumber, about ¼ in/6 mm square and 7½ in/19 cm long

California Roll

As we explained earlier, the California roll was invented in Los Angeles by a Japanese sushi chef who was trying to come up with ways to use the ingredients available in his new home. Eventually it became an inside-out roll (*uramaki*), as well, because the chef felt that American diners preferred the texture of the rice over that of the nori on the outside of the roll.

½ sheet nori, toasted (see page 112)

Hand water (see page 113)

¾ cup/120 g sushi rice (see page 105) at body temperature, covered with a damp kitchen towel

2 tsp sesame seeds, toasted (see page 34)

¼ tsp wasabi

¼ Hass avocado, peeled

¼ cup/50 g crabmeat, picked over for shell fragments

1 piece Japanese cucumber, about ¼ in/6 mm square and 7½ in/19 cm long

Soy sauce for serving

Place a bamboo sushi mat, shiny-side up, on your work surface, with the bamboo sticks running horizontally. Cut a piece of plastic wrap large enough to cover the mat loosely and place it over the mat. (The plastic wrap prevents the rice from sticking to the mat.)

Place the nori sheet, rough-side up and with a long side facing you, at the bottom edge of the mat. Moisten the palm of one hand lightly with the hand water, then rub your hands together to moisten them. Pick up the rice and place it on the center of the nori sheet. Moisten your hands again and gently spread the rice, creating a layer of rice covering the entire sheet and being careful not to compress the rice too much.

Sprinkle the sesame seeds evenly over the rice. Flip the nori sheet upside down so the rice is now facing down. Use your index finger to scoop up the wasabi and smear it horizontally across the center of the nori. Cut the avocado quarter in half lengthwise. Place the pieces, horizontally, in the center of the nori sheet, with the fat end of one piece to the

left, the fat end of the other piece to the right, and the thin ends meeting in the middle. Place the crabmeat on the avocado, distributing it evenly, and then top the crabmeat with the cucumber.

Working from the edge of the mat nearest you, place your thumbs near the corners of the mat and start to roll, lifting up the corners of the mat and using your fingers along the front edge to flip the rice up and over the filling away from you. Complete the roll by meeting the front edge of the roll to the rice at the end of the nori. Hold the roll in place while pulling back gently on the rolled portion of the mat to tighten. Continue rolling, always keeping the roll snug so the fillings stay in place, until you reach the far end of the rice. Hold the mat to tighten again, pulling slightly toward you, to seal.

Position the finished roll horizontally on a dry cutting board. Place the tip of your slicing knife into the hand water, then lift the tip up vertically to moisten the length of the blade. With the moistened blade, cut the roll in half crosswise. Place the halves horizontally side by side, hold them together with one hand, and slice them crosswise into thirds to create six equal-size pieces. If the knife becomes sticky between cuts, wipe the blade with a moist towel to remove the rice and moisten the blade again before the next cut.

Arrange the rolls on a plate, with some pieces standing on their sides and others lying down, and serve with soy sauce.

Lobster Roll

This is not exactly the New England version and not exactly the well-known 101 roll, but it is possibly more delicious than either of them. This sushi takes a bit of effort: you have to cook, cool, and shell the lobster before you use it. The good news is that you can complete those steps much earlier in the day or even the day before. And if lobster is not in your budget, you can use two large prawns. If you don't want to fry the lobster, just slice and garnish as directed after the fry instructions.

This is a good technique to learn because many other fillings can be treated the same way; some of the more unusual rolls that you encounter in sushi restaurants are examples of this.

6 qt/5.7 L water

3 tbsp kosher salt

One 1-lb/455-g live lobster

¼ Hass avocado, peeled and cut into ¼-in/6-mm cubes

2 tbsp mayonnaise

2 tsp flying fish roe

½ tsp white miso

Vegetable oil for deep-frying

1 sheet nori, toasted (see page 112)

Hand water (see page 113)

¾ cup/120 g sushi rice (see page 105) at body temperature, covered with a damp kitchen towel

BATTER

2 tbsp all-purpose flour

2 tbsp rice flour

2 tbsp cornstarch

⅛ tsp baking powder

Pinch of kosher salt

5 tbsp/75 ml cold soda water

1 tsp soy glaze (page 118)

½ tsp mayonnaise

½ tsp flying fish roe

Soy sauce for serving

In a large stockpot, bring the water and salt to a boil over high heat. Have ready a large bowl of ice water. Carefully lower the lobster into the boiling water. After the water returns to a boil, lower the heat to medium and cook for 5 minutes. Using tongs or a wire skimmer, transfer the lobster to the ice water to cool. When the lobster has cooled completely, remove it from the ice water, twist off its head, and place the head in a bowl. The head contains the tomalley, which is part of the digestive system, and it will be either yellowish green or a dark green. It looks a bit homely but it tastes great, and it adds a lot of flavor to the lobster roll. Remove the tomalley from the head and place it on a paper towel to absorb the excess moisture. Discard the head.

Lay the tail on its side and press down on it with a flattened hand until you hear the shell crack. This should break the shell away from the meat. Remove the meat from the claw and the knuckle with a lobster cracker, or use kitchen scissors to cut open the claw and knuckle shells. Slice the tail meat from the thicker side of the tail into 8 medallions, each ³⁄₁₆ in/5 mm thick. Set aside for garnish. Dice the remaining meat into ¼-in/6-mm cubes.

In a small bowl, combine the cubed lobster meat, avocado, mayonnaise, roe, miso, and tomalley and stir to mix well.

Pour the oil to a depth of at least 2½ in/6 cm in a heavy saucepan 10 in/25 cm in diameter and at least 5 in/12 cm deep and heat to 350°F/180°C on a deep-frying thermometer. Place a wire rack on a baking sheet.

While the oil is heating, make the roll. Place a bamboo sushi mat, shiny-side up, on your work surface, with the bamboo sticks running horizontally. The mat should be completely dry so that the nori remains dry and crisp. Place the nori sheet, rough-side up and a long side facing you, on the mat.

Moisten the palm of one hand lightly with the hand water, then rub your hands together to moisten them. Pick up the rice and place it on the center of the nori sheet. Moisten your hands again, and using just your fingertips, spread the rice using a gentle pinching motion. It is important not to smash or compress the rice, as you want it to stay fluffy. Create an even layer of rice covering almost the entire nori sheet, leaving ½ in/12 mm uncovered at the long edge farthest from you. Remoisten your hands as necessary to keep the rice from sticking to your fingers, but be careful not to use too much water or the rice will lose its stickiness. Using your fingertips, pinch the rice to create a low, narrow ridge of rice along the front edge nearest you. This will keep the filling in place.

Spoon the lobster mixture horizontally across the rice just inside the ridge. Put one hand on each side of the nori sheet and, with your thumbs under the near corners of the mat, start to roll, lifting up the edge of the mat and immediately moving your hands along the front edge to flip the nori up and over the filling away from you. Complete the roll by meeting the front edge of the roll to the rice. Hold the nori in place while pulling back gently on the rolled portion of the mat to tighten. Continue rolling, always keeping the roll snug so the filling stays in place, until you reach the far end of the nori. Hold the mat to tighten again, pulling slightly toward you, to seal. Reserve the finished roll.

To make the batter: In a small bowl, whisk together the all-purpose flour, rice flour, cornstarch, baking powder, and salt. Slowly whisk in the soda water. Transfer the batter to a pan in which the lobster roll can lie flat.

Dip the lobster roll in the batter and roll it to cover completely. Carefully lower the roll into the hot oil and deep-fry until the batter becomes crunchy, about

1 minute. You don't want to cook the roll too long because you want the filling to stay cold. Using the wire skimmer, carefully transfer the roll to the wire rack to drain.

Position the finished roll horizontally on a dry cutting board. Place the tip of your slicing knife into the hand water, then lift the tip up vertically to moisten the length of the blade. With the moistened blade, cut the roll in half crosswise. Place the halves horizontally side by side, hold them together with one hand, and slice them crosswise into quarters to create eight equal-size pieces. If the knife becomes sticky between cuts, wipe the blade with a moist towel to remove the rice and moisten the blade again before the next cut.

Drizzle the glaze on a serving plate, and arrange the pieces, cut-side up, on the glaze. Place a lobster medallion on each slice. Spoon a dot of the mayonnaise on the center of each lobster medallion, and sprinkle the roe evenly over the mayonnaise. Serve with soy sauce.

How to

Make Temaki (Hand Rolls)

Temaki are easy to make. Even if you make a mistake, you can unroll the nori and fix it or add an ingredient you may have forgotten. Almost anything that you would put into a traditional maki, you can put into a temaki. Hand rolls are also great party food. You can set up all the different filling ingredients on plates and in bowls. Toast a pile of nori sheets and stack them, make a bowl of sushi rice, and have your friends roll their own (no, not 1960s-style). It is fun and interesting to see what people put in their temaki. If you like, for serving, purchase one or more temaki holders, which are platform-like stands in wood, lacquer, plastic, or other material with holes for holding the rolls upright.

MAKES 1 TEMAKI

½ sheet nori, toasted (see page 112)

Hand water (see page 113)

¼ cup/40 g sushi rice (see page 105) at body temperature, covered with a damp kitchen towel

Wasabi, as specified in individual recipes

Ingredient(s) for filling roll, as specified in individual recipes

Hold the nori sheet, shiny-side down, in your left hand (if you are left-handed, reverse the directions for left and right hands), securing it in place with your left thumb on top and supporting its length with your fingers. Moisten your right hand with the hand water and pick up the sushi rice. Gently gather the rice into a loose ball in your hand, then press the rice onto the left half of the nori. Spread the rice about ¼ in/6 mm thick, leaving a border of the nori on the top, bottom, and left side uncovered. The right half of the nori should not have any rice on it (1). Using your right index finger, gently press the middle of the rice to make an indentation on the diagonal (the angle should be from the left top corner of the nori to the middle of the bottom length). Use your right index finger to smear the wasabi on the indentation.

Place the ingredients on the indentation in the rice (2). Bring the bottom left corner of the nori to the middle of the nori sheet (3), so that the midpoint of the bottom of the nori becomes the point of the cone (4). Roll the nori around the ingredients and sushi rice (5). When you complete the roll, it should be a tight cone (6). If you are laying the roll down to serve it, place it seam-side down.

1

2

3

4

Make Temaki (Hand Rolls)

5

6

Temaki with Salmon Skin (Sake no Kawa)

When salmon skin is toasted, it develops a delicious deep-roasted flavor and a richness from the little bit of salmon flesh that remains on the skin. This hand roll is crispy both from the nori and the salmon skin. You can use skin from any of the salmon family, including ocean trout. Another good option is the skin from smoked salmon, which will have a more robust flavor. When using any fish skin, however, you must make sure that all the scales have been removed. If a little flesh is clinging to the skin after you have filleted a salmon, leave it there for the extra flavor it will deliver. Salmon skin is often thrown away by fishmongers, so if you have a good relationship with your fishmonger, ask him or her to save you the salmon skin that would otherwise be discarded. Do make sure it doesn't have scales. Whether the skin comes from your own efforts filleting a salmon or from your fishmonger, you can roll it up, wrap it tightly in plastic wrap, and freeze it for about a month, then thaw it slowly in the refrigerator before using.

⅛ tsp kosher salt

1 oz/30 g salmon skin without scales, with attached flesh ¼ in/6 mm thick

1 tbsp vegetable oil

½ sheet nori, toasted (see page 112)

¼ cup/40 g sushi rice (see page 105) at body temperature, covered with a damp kitchen towel

¼ tsp wasabi

⅛ tsp sesame seeds, toasted (see page 34)

1 tsp coarsely chopped pickled turnip (see page 158), patted dry

10 daikon sprouts, roots removed

1 tsp salmon roe

Soy sauce for serving

Sprinkle the salt evenly over both sides of the salmon skin, cover, and refrigerate for 3 hours. Remove the skin from the refrigerator and pat dry with a paper towel. Using a sharp knife, cut the skin into long strips ¼ in/6 mm wide.

In a small skillet, heat the oil over medium heat. Add the skin strips and cook until golden brown and crispy, about 1½ minutes. Transfer the strips to a paper towel, top with a second towel, and pat dry. Coarsely chop the strips.

Following the directions for How to Make Temaki (page 198), hold the nori, spread the rice on it, make the indentation, and then smear the wasabi on the indentation. Sprinkle the sesame seeds evenly over the rice. Arrange the salmon skin and pickled turnip in the indentation and position the daikon sprouts with the green leaves sticking out from the top of the nori. Roll up the nori as directed, then spoon the salmon roe on top. Serve with soy sauce.

Temaki with Spicy Tuna (Piri-kara Maguro)

The amount of spiciness is up to your personal taste. Here we have used a favorite Thai hot sauce. You can use any hot sauce you prefer, or you can add chopped fresh chiles. This hand roll is good made with almost any type of seafood you can chop, from octopus to shrimp to sea bass.

3 tbsp chopped tuna

½ tsp mayonnaise

½ tsp flying fish roe

¼ tsp Sriracha sauce

¼ tsp finely chopped green onion, white part only or white and tender green part

½ sheet nori, toasted (see page 112)

¼ cup/40 g sushi rice (see page 105) at body temperature, covered with a damp kitchen towel

⅛ tsp wasabi

10 daikon sprouts, roots removed

Soy sauce for serving

In a small bowl, combine the tuna, mayonnaise, roe, Sriracha sauce, and green onion and stir to mix. Following the directions for How to Make Temaki (page 198), make 1 roll with the nori, rice, and wasabi, arranging the tuna mixture in the indentation. Roll up the nori as directed, tuck in the daikon sprouts with the green leaves sticking out from the top, and serve with soy sauce.

Sushi Bowls
(Sushi Don)

and Other Types of Sushi

Sushi Bowl with Chopped Tuna and Green Onion (Maguro Negi Don)

We often make this at home. It all starts with a call from Hiro to "put the rice on." When Hiro arrives, Lissa never knows what he has, but if it is the bits and pieces from trimming tuna, she knows exactly what to do. If you have the sinewy part of the tuna, this is a very quick dish. All you need to do is gently scrape the meat off the sinew. As it comes away, it is already chopped for using. By the time Hiro comes back to the kitchen, Lissa has the tuna ready to put in the bowls. Raw egg yolk is not for everyone, but if you trust your eggs and want to try it, it will give the tuna a richness and lusciousness that is addictive.

2½ cups/625 g chopped tuna

2 tsp chopped green onion, white part only or white and tender green part

½ sheet nori, toasted (see page 112)

8 cups/1.3 kg sushi rice (see page 105) at body temperature, covered with a damp kitchen towel

4 egg yolks from cage-free chickens (optional)

4 shiso leaves for garnish (optional)

3 tbsp pickled ginger (see page 120), squeezed to release excess moisture (optional)

1 tbsp wasabi

Soy sauce for serving

Have ready four donburi or other small bowls. In a mixing bowl, combine the tuna and green onion and toss to mix well. Using kitchen scissors or a very sharp knife, cut the nori into strips ⅛ in/3 mm wide and 1½ in/4 cm long.

Put 2 cups/320 g of the rice into each bowl. Sprinkle the nori evenly over the rice. Divide the tuna mixture into 4 equal portions, and shape each portion into a disk 3½ in/9 cm in diameter. Place a disk on the center of each serving of rice. If using the egg yolks, with the back of a spoon, gently make a shallow indentation in the middle of the tuna in each bowl, and place a yolk in each indentation. Garnish with a shiso leaf, if desired. Divide the pickled ginger (if using) and wasabi evenly among the bowls, placing it next to the tuna. Serve with soy sauce.

Sushi Bowl with Soy-marinated Tuna (Maguro no Zuke Don)

In this version of a tuna sushi bowl, the tuna slices are marinated in a soy mixture to give them a special flavor created by the chef. Quick and easy, this dish is very popular in Japan, especially at lunchtime. This bowl is also very good made with just beautifully sliced tuna, which you can serve with soy sauce for dipping.

SOY MARINADE

4½ tsp sake

4½ tsp mirin

3 tbsp dashi (see page 114)

3 tbsp soy sauce

36 slices tuna loin, each 3 by 1 by ⅜ in/7.5 by 2.5 by 1 cm (see How to Slice Tuna for Nigiri, page 81, if starting with a steak or large loin; if not, see How to Slice Bonito for Nigiri, page 80)

½ sheet nori, toasted (see page 112)

8 cups/1.3 kg sushi rice (see page 105) at body temperature, covered with a damp kitchen towel

4 tbsp/50 g pickled ginger (see page 120), squeezed to release excess moisture

4 tsp wasabi

Soy sauce for serving

Have ready four donburi or other small bowls.

To make the soy marinade: In a medium-size bowl, combine the sake, mirin, dashi, and soy sauce and mix well.

Add the tuna slices to the marinade, turn to mix gently, and let stand for 3 minutes. Meanwhile, using kitchen scissors or a very sharp knife, cut the nori into strips ⅛ in/3 mm wide and 1½ in/4 cm long.

Put 2 cups/320 g of the rice into each bowl. Sprinkle the nori evenly over the rice. Remove the tuna from the marinade. Dividing the tuna slices evenly, arrange them over the nori like flower petals, fanning them out from the center of the bowl. Divide the pickled ginger evenly among the bowls, placing it in the center of each bowl. Divide the wasabi evenly and place it on top of the ginger. Serve with soy sauce.

Sushi Bowl with Wild Salmon and Salmon Roe (Sake Ikura Don)

Sometimes this sushi bowl of salmon and salmon roe is called "mother and child." The salmon eggs add a nice pop when you eat one or two with a piece of the salmon. This dish is especially good when prepared with one of the fattier species of wild salmon, such as king salmon or Copper River salmon. (See page 133 for a precaution on serving raw salmon.)

½ sheet nori, toasted (see page 112)

8 cups/1.3 kg sushi rice (see page 105) at body temperature, covered with a damp kitchen towel

2 shiso leaves, julienned

36 slices salmon fillet, each 3 by 1 by ¼ in/7.5 cm by 2.5 cm by 6 mm (see How to Slice Round Fish Fillet for Nigiri, page 64)

6 tbsp/115 g salmon roe

3 tbsp pickled ginger (see page 120), squeezed to release excess moisture

4 tsp wasabi

Soy sauce for serving

Have ready four donburi or other small bowls. Using kitchen scissors or a very sharp knife, cut the nori into strips ⅛ in/3 mm wide and 1½ in/4 cm long.

Put 2 cups/320 g of the rice into each bowl. Sprinkle the nori evenly over the rice, followed by the shiso. Dividing the salmon slices evenly, arrange them over the nori and shiso like flower petals, fanning them out from the center of the bowl. Using the back of a spoon, make a small indentation in the center of the salmon and rice in each bowl. Spoon 1½ tbsp of the salmon roe into each indentation. Divide the pickled ginger and wasabi evenly among the bowls, placing the ginger on one side of the salmon and the wasabi on the other. Serve with soy sauce.

Sushi Bowl with Sea Urchin and Salmon Roe (Uni Ikura Don)

This is a luxurious dish, with the sea urchin (*uni*) contributing a rich creaminess and the salmon roe (*ikura*) delivering a burst of saltiness with each bite. It is also pleasing to the eye, because of the different shades of orange. If you like, you can customize each bowl, using more or less uni or ikura depending on your diners' preferences. Although good-quality ikura is typically easy to find, you might want to try a different kind of roe. The closest in flavor to salmon roe is ocean trout roe, which is almost the same color but a bit smaller. Many different types of flying fish roe (*tobiko*) exist, as well, with orange tobiko being the most common. You might also try mixing two or three different types.

½ **sheet nori, toasted (see page 112)**

8 **cups/1.3 kg sushi rice (see page 105) at body temperature, covered with a damp kitchen cloth**

2 **shiso leaves, julienned**

24 **tongues sea urchin roe, about 7 oz/200 g**

6 **tbsp/115 g salmon roe**

4 **egg yolks from cage-free chickens (optional)**

3 **tbsp pickled ginger (see page 120), squeezed to release excess moisture**

4 **tsp wasabi**

Soy sauce for serving

Have ready four donburi or other small bowls. Using kitchen scissors or a very sharp knife, cut the nori into strips ⅛ in/3 mm wide and 1½ in/4 cm long.

Put 2 cups/320 g of the rice into each bowl. Sprinkle the nori evenly over the rice, followed by the shiso. Dividing the sea urchin roe evenly, place it over the nori and shiso, arranging it in a circle on the rice. Dividing the salmon roe evenly, place it inside the sea urchin circle, leaving the center empty. If using the egg yolks, make a shallow indentation in the center of each rice bowl and place an egg yolk in the indentation. Divide the pickled ginger and wasabi evenly among the bowls, placing them outside the sea urchin circle. Serve with soy sauce.

Scattered Sushi (Chirashi-zushi)

Chirashi-zushi is arguably the easiest style of sushi to master. Once you are comfortable making sushi rice, all you need to do is top it with an assortment of ingredients of your choice, traditionally a combination of a few kinds of seafood, seasoned vegetables, seasoned omelet, pickled ginger, and wasabi. Part of the appeal of this dish is the decorative way the ingredients are laid in the bowl. You should try to arrange them so that contrasting colors are overlapping one another and textural items are placed randomly but not next to one another.

8 cups/1.3 kg sushi rice (see page 105) at body temperature, covered with a damp kitchen towel

½ sheet nori, toasted (see page 112), cut into ½-in/12-mm squares

4 cleaned sea scallops, about 1½ oz/45 g each, each cut in half horizontally (see Note)

8 slices tuna loin, each 3 by 1 by ⅜ in/7.5 by 2.5 by 1 cm (see How to Slice Tuna for Nigiri, page 81, if starting with a steak or large loin; if not, see How to Slice Bonito for Nigiri, page 80)

8 Dungeness crab legs, cooked and shelled

8 slices amberjack, each 3 by 1 by ¼ in/7.5 cm by 2.5 cm by 6 mm

8 tongues sea urchin roe, about 2¼ oz/65 g

4 slices Dashi-flavored Rolled Omelet (page 116), each ¾ in/2 cm thick

4 tbsp/75 salmon roe

2 shiso leaves, cut in half lengthwise and then cut into fine julienne

3 tbsp pickled ginger (see page 120)

4 tsp wasabi

Soy sauce for serving

Have ready four donburi or other small bowls. Put 2 cups/320 g of the rice into each bowl and sprinkle the nori evenly over the rice. Divide the scallops, tuna, crab legs, amberjack, sea urchin, omelet, and salmon roe into four equal portions, and put one portion of each over the rice and nori in each bowl. Sprinkle the shiso evenly over the top. Place one-fourth each of the pickled ginger and wasabi to one side of each bowl. Serve with soy sauce.

Note: See Nigiri with Sea Scallops (page 147) for directions on working with fresh scallops in the shell and thawed frozen scallops.

Bouzushi with Vinegar-cured Mackerel (Shime Saba)

Bouzushi means "rod sushi" or "stick sushi" and usually refers to rolling a whole side of a fish fillet around sushi rice. The roll ends up being a rod about 8 in/20 cm long by 3 in/7.5 cm in diameter. Kyoto is famous for bouzushi made with vinegar-cured mackerel, where the rolls are sold enclosed in a bamboo wrapper for takeout. The bamboo, along with the vinegar, is thought to help kill unwanted bacteria.

This is our twist on the traditional bouzushi. Just before we serve it, we use a kitchen torch to brown the skin of the fish, which slightly warms the fish at the same time. The contrast of the warm fish, toasty skin, and vinegared rice goes together especially well. This sushi does not require soy sauce for serving.

Two 4-oz/115-g fillets Vinegar-cured Mackerel (page 104)

1 tsp wasabi

2 tsp green nori powder

Hand water (see page 113)

1½ cups/240 g sushi rice (see page 105) at body temperature, covered with a damp kitchen towel

2 tsp peeled and very finely julienned fresh ginger

Place a bamboo sushi mat, shiny-side up, on your work surface, with the bamboo sticks running horizontally. Cut a piece of plastic wrap large enough to cover the mat loosely. Cover the mat with the plastic wrap.

Carefully peel off the silver skin from each fillet. To ensure it comes up easily, start from the thicker end and pull across the fillet. Score the skinned side of each fillet on the diagonal in a ¼-in/6-mm diamond pattern. Place the fillets, flesh-side up and horizontally, on the prepared mat, positioning them end to end and about one-third above the edge of the mat closest to you. Smear the wasabi on the fillets and then sprinkle the fillets with the nori powder.

Moisten the palm of one hand lightly with the hand water, then rub your hands together to moisten them. Pick up the rice and shape it into a rod the length of the fish, moistening your hands as needed to prevent the rice from sticking to them. Place the rod of rice horizontally on top of the fillet. Lift up the bottom and top edge of the plastic wrap and bring them together to meet, creating a sling for the fillet and rice and

fusing the fillet and rice together. Lift the edge of the sushi mat closest to you up and over to cover the fish and rice, then start to roll away from you, pressing the mat tightly and pushing inward at the same time to keep the roll uniform. Position the finished roll so the rice is on the bottom and the fish is on the top. Using the sushi mat, press the rod of rice and fish into a brick shape, then tighten the mat. Let rest at room temperature for 30 minutes.

Set the bouzushi on a cutting board and unwrap from the plastic wrap. Place the piece of plastic wrap over the top and sides of the bouzushi, leaving the bottom uncovered and resting on the cutting board. Gently press the top and two sides with the sushi mat, then remove the mat and cut the roll through the plastic wrap crosswise into slices 1 in/2.5 cm thick. The plastic wrap will help keep the fish and rice together as you cut. Remove the plastic wrap and, with a kitchen torch, sear the skin until it is light brown. Garnish each piece of sushi with julienned ginger before serving.

Stuffed Sushi in a Soybean Pouch (Inari-zushi)

Hiro's mother used to make *inari-zushi* (sushi rice in a soybean pouch) for him and his brother for special occasions, and every time he eats one, it brings back sweet memories. The sushi shares its name with Inari, the Shinto god of rice, fertility, agriculture, and more, and with the many shrines in Japan dedicated to the versatile divinity. We recommend serving pickled vegetables, such as the turnip on page 158 or sunomono, alongside this sushi to complement its mild sweetness.

To make these stuffed pouches, you will need to purchase slices of fried tofu, or *aburagé*, which are available frozen, in cans, and in the fresh-food section of Japanese and other Asian markets and in well-stocked supermarkets. If you can find only square aburagé, you can cut them on the diagonal to make triangular pouches. Preseasoned pouches are available, and if you are pressed for time, they work perfectly. The seasoning, however, is a bit different from homemade and is not as satisfying. Because the pouches are well seasoned, the sushi does not require soy sauce or wasabi for serving.

2 cups/480 ml water

2 slices fried tofu, about 4 by 3 in/10 by 7.5 cm

4 tsp soy sauce

2 tbsp sugar

½ cup/120 ml dashi (see page 114)

¾ cup/120 g sushi rice (see page 105) at body temperature, covered with a damp kitchen towel

In a medium-size saucepan, bring the water to a boil. Have ready a medium-size bowl of cold water. Meanwhile, cut the tofu slices crosswise to create four 2-by-3-in/5-by-7.5-cm pouches. Gently open the pouches.

Slip the pouches into the boiling water and blanch for 3 seconds, then drain, immerse in the bowl of cold water, and squeeze gently to remove the excess oil.

In a small saucepan, stir together the soy sauce, sugar, and dashi, then add the pouches. Place a lid, small plate, or disk of parchment paper that fits just inside the pan on the surface of the liquid. This is to keep the pouches submerged in the cooking liquid. Cook for

5 minutes, rotating the pouches in the cooking liquid a couple of times as they cook. Remove from the heat and let cool to room temperature in the cooking liquid.

Just before you are ready to stuff the pouches, squeeze out the excess—but not all—liquid from the pouches. The remaining liquid is part of the seasoning of the sushi.

Following the directions for How to Make Sushi Rice Balls (page 108), make 4 rice balls. Carefully place a rice ball in each pouch. (Work slowly and gently, as the pouches tear easily). Close the open end by simply folding the ends and sides over the rice. Place the pouch, closed-side down, on a serving plate. This sushi will keep on the counter for up to 6 hours before serving. Once refrigerated, it is difficult to bring the pouches to room temperature, which is necessary to return the rice to a good soft texture.

Variation: You can mix other ingredients into the sushi rice to make your own style of inari-zushi. Among the possibilities are pickled ginger (see page 120), peas, chives, small shrimp, or preserved dashi kombu (see Note, page 114). Or, instead of closing the pouch, you can top the rice in the pouch with your favorite ingredients, such as shrimp, crabmeat, peas, or most vegetables, to make a Japanese-style open-face sandwich. Use your imagination. Any pouches that contain fish or shellfish should be eaten immediately, however, and not left on the counter for serving later.

Note: The tofu pouches can be cooked and cooled up to 24 hours ahead of time, refrigerated in their cooling liquid. Bring to room temperature before using.

Sushi Rice–stuffed Monterey Squid (Ika) with Sea Urchin (Uni)

This is a faux roll, or maybe a new version of formed sushi. Whichever way you think about it, the presentation is beautiful and the dish is very easy to make. The whiteness of the squid is particularly stunning paired with the vivid orange of the sea urchin, but if you are just not an uni person, the dish is still delicious without it. We prefer to buy whole fresh Monterey squid, but they are seasonal and difficult to find. Most fish markets carry uncleaned whole squid and cleaned whole squid. Either can be used here, but make sure the squid is sushi grade before you purchase it. Because it can be difficult to find the exact-size squid needed for this recipe, you may need a little more or a little less rice than called for here.

4 whole squid, each body about 4 in/10 cm long without the tentacles

½ cup/80 g sushi rice (see page 105) at body temperature, covered with a damp kitchen towel

¼ tsp peeled and grated fresh ginger

8 tongues sea urchin roe, each about 1½ in/4 cm long (see Note)

Soy sauce for serving

Following the directions for How to Break Down Squid (page 100), clean the squid, reserving the whole bodies and the tentacles.

Heat a charcoal or gas grill or a stove-top grill pan to medium-high; you should be able to hold your palm 4 in/10 cm above the heat for no more than 5 seconds.

Following the directions for How to Make Sushi Rice Balls (page 108), make 4 rice balls. Shape a rice ball into a log about ¼ in/6 mm in diameter and the length of the squid body. Stuff the rice into the squid body. To close the squid body, weave a toothpick through the open end of the body parallel to the opening. Repeat with the remaining rice balls and squid bodies.

If using a grill, place a grill screen on the rack for the tentacles. Place the stuffed squid and tentacles on the grill rack or pan and grill, turning as necessary, until golden brown on all sides, about 3 minutes total. You want the squid to get a little char and smokiness. Do not overcook the squid or it will be chewy.

Remove the squid and tentacles from the grill or pan and let rest for about 20 seconds, then cut each body in half crosswise. Remove the toothpicks and arrange the bodies and tentacles attractively on a serving plate. Place a dab of the ginger on top of each body portion, and place the sea urchin on the top of the ginger. Serve with soy sauce.

Note: If the sea urchin tongues are longer than 1½ in/4 cm, cut each one in half crosswise.

Index